PADDLES & WHEELS

PADDLES & WHEELS

Everyday Life and Travel in Canada

by

L. M. Grayson
and
J. Paul Grayson

CONSULTANTS

P. Kettle
and
M. Halloran

Toronto
Oxford University Press
1974

Cover, design, and drawings by FRED HUFFMAN

© Oxford University Press (Canadian Branch) 1974

ISBN-0-19-540216-2

Printed in Canada by
THE BRYANT PRESS LIMITED

Contents

Preface

It is difficult to find appropriate words to thank those who have assisted in the preparation of a book. It is especially difficult in this case because much of the credit belongs to Ms Tilly Crawley of Oxford University Press. Without her enthusiasm and concrete suggestions, *Paddles and Wheels* might never have been written. In addition, Ms Crawley formulated many of the questions for discussion that appear at the end of this volume.

We would also like to thank Shirley Marshall who typed the manuscript through its numerous revisions and painstakingly tracked down all the photographs that appear in the text.

LMG
JPG

1 Canoes and Snowshoes

In the beginning there was nothing but water, nothing but a wide, wide sea. The only creatures in the world were the animals who lived in and on the water. Then down from the sky world a woman fell, a divine person. Two loons flying over the water placed themselves beneath her and joined their bodies to make a cushion for her to rest upon.

The Great Turtle sent the Beaver, Muskrat, and Toad to dive to the bottom of the sea and bring up some earth. The woman took the earth and it grew larger and larger until it formed a great country where trees and other plants could live and flourish.

After some time the woman gave birth to twins. And so began the life of man on earth, according to Huron legend.

Through the years the Huron Indians learned to live on this land, which was covered by thick forests and clear, fresh rivers, lakes, and streams. They planted crops, gathered wild berries, hunted for deer, and fished for sturgeon and trout. Life was difficult and as unpredictable as the seasons of the year. Everyone was expected to contribute to the prosperity of the tribe and laziness was not tolerated.

The Hurons, who lived in what is now central Ontario, were one of the most developed tribes in Canada. They lived in villages and used the land to cultivate corn, beans, squash, and tobacco. A strict division

Indian women cultivating corn.
*What might the men have been doing while the
women were working in the fields?*

of labour ensured that each member of the tribe was kept busy. During the early spring the women gathered firewood for cooking for the coming months when the trees would be too green to burn. If they could not find trees that were quite dry, they felled ones that had dry branches and broke these into splinters. In the spring, summer, and fall the women spent much of their time in the fields. They tilled the ground; planted and harvested the corn; stored it; and prepared it for eating. During the long winter months the women and young girls made the mats of reeds that were used both to hang in the doors and to sit on. They dressed and softened the skins of beaver, moose, and other animals. Leather game bags and tobacco pouches were sewn and decorated with red, black, white, and blue porcupine quills. Reeds and birch bark were the basic materials used to make baskets and bowls that would later hold corn, meat, fish, and other foods.

During times of plenty the Huron usually had two meals a day, one in the morning and the other in the early evening. The women

Indian containers made of birch bark.
Spruce root fibres, dyed in various colours, were
used to sew the containers.

prepared the meals by pounding or grinding corn between two stones. The corn was then roasted in hot ashes or ground into mush and mixed with water. Sometimes a little rotten or powdered fish was added for extra flavour.

For feasts and celebrations the Huron women prepared a special dish called 'stinking corn'. To make it they put a number of ears of unripe corn into a muddy pool of stagnant water for two or three months. The corn was then removed and boiled with meat or fish. Even the bread that was used to supplement their daily diet was made from ground corn, boiled in water and kneaded into dough. Since they did not have yeast, the loaves were flat and usually not longer than two inches. In the summer fresh fruits such as raspberries, blueberries, or strawberries might be added to the top of the bread.

When game was scarce corn was the only food that stood between the Indian and starvation. Thus it was essential not to waste even one kernel. Since corn was so important to the Hurons and other Indian tribes of the eastern and middle sections of the North American continent, it is not surprising that many stories, songs, and festivals were dedicated to the great Spirit of Corn. One legend of the Iroquois tribes claims that it was the Crow who first carried a grain of corn to the

Indian in order to save the people from starvation when the hunt was unsuccessful. Another tells of a young Iroquois brave who went out to hunt after his wife had deserted him. After wandering through the forest for a long time he reached a small hill where a lovely young maid sat alone. He approached the girl and enquired where she had come from and why she sat alone. The girl quietly explained that she had come from heaven to provide food for the poor people. She then sent the young hunter away after making him promise to return to the same spot in twelve moons. When he returned the hill was laden with corn, squash, and tobacco as far as the eye could see.

An Ojibway legend stresses that once, a very long time ago, there was a band of Indians who had been blessed with a large, healthy crop of corn. They had so much that they became wasteful, fed it to their dogs, and allowed much of it to rot in the fields. This waste saddened and angered the good Spirit of Corn who heaped misfortune on these ungrateful wretches. A wise man from the village roamed through the forest while he decided what should be done. At last he made a sacrifice to the good Spirit of Corn and opened his heart to the suggestions of this great Spirit. In the end he promised that his people would use their crops wisely and carefully in the future if only they were spared more grief. The good Spirit heard his prayers and had pity on his people. When the next harvest came the people took great care to thank the good Spirit and to avoid all wastefulness.

While the Huron women did most of what we might consider the hard work, the Huron men spent a great deal of their time fishing and hunting. In the early spring and summer they would set out for nearby lakes and rivers in their canoes, with large nets to catch fish. In the fall many travelled by canoe to the deep waters of Lake Huron where they made camp on one of the small islands close to the fishing grounds. During the trip to Lake Huron fish hooks made of sharpened bone and baited with frog's skin were attached to the back of the canoe. Fish caught by this method were usually eaten when camp was made at the end of each day. Once the islands of Lake Huron had been reached, small groups built a temporary shelter around a common campfire. Every evening the Hurons took their nets by canoe into the open lake and fished all night. At daybreak they returned and divided the catch

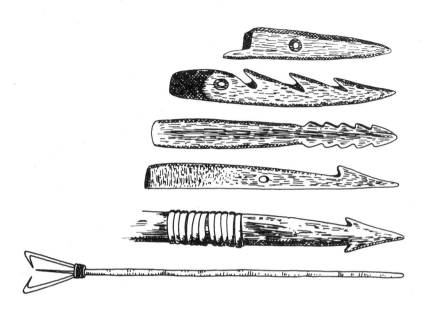

Bone fish spears.

of sturgeon and trout among everyone who had helped. To preserve the fish the Hurons usually dried or smoked them almost immediately. If the fishing was unsuccessful the Hurons often travelled to the Algonkin camps, which were located to the north and west of the St Lawrence in the area drained by the Ottawa River. Here they would trade corn and tobacco for fish.

Unlike fishing, which was confined primarily to the warmer months of spring through fall, hunting was important all year. Indians were often faced with a scarcity of game. Few animals ventured near their camps and the hunters were forced to travel many miles to make the hunt a success. If moose or deer were plentiful the most usual method of hunting was the animal drive. One group of hunters would run through the forest shouting and making much noise to frighten the animals and drive them into the open where they were either met by

Building a birch-bark canoe.
What purpose do the wooden slats serve?

another group of armed hunters; or, if the clearing bordered on a river or stream, the hunters would sit in their canoes at the water's edge waiting for the bewildered animals to show themselves. As soon as the animals were spotted, the hunters hurled long poles that had sharpened blades attached to one end. In addition to deer and moose, many tribes also ate bears, rabbits, wild turkeys, and dogs. In fact dogs were raised by some Indians for many of the same reasons that Europeans kept flocks of sheep.

While the Indian women usually remained in the camp, the men had to travel long distances to fish, trade, and hunt. Without horses or carts and with no roads to travel on, the trips were long, difficult, and often dangerous. During the summer months the Hurons, for example, found that the birch-bark canoe was the safest, swiftest, and by far the easiest way of moving men and supplies from one place to another.

The Algonkins, who lived in the Ottawa-St Lawrence region, were especially noted for their skill in building this craft. Depending largely on hunting for their food, they had to be able to move quickly. They would spend only a few days at a time in one place before moving on, and in summer birch-bark canoes made travel easy. The Algonkins

Shooting the rapids.
What features of the canoe made travel in shallow, rocky streams possible?
What disadvantages did the birch-bark canoe have when navigating those streams?

relied solely on what nature provided to construct their canoes. The bark of the birch tree was the best material for the shell of the canoe. But sometimes spruce bark, elm bark, or moose hides were used. Since birch bark does not readily strip from the tree until early summer, most canoes were built in June.

One explorer described the skill with which the Indian had learned to strip bark from the birch tree.

The tree being smooth is difficult to ascend, and for his purpose the Native ties a strong leather cord to the great toes of his feet, leaving a space between them of about one foot, and having a strong square-headed knife, very sharp at the point, in his belt, he ascends the tree to as far as the Rind is good, then raising a small strip from around the tree, in a straight line downwards cuts quite through the rind, which readily leaves the bark, and while the sap is rising comes off so freely that two persons with light poles keep it to the tree until it can be carefully taken down; it is then warmed and its circular form made flat, laid on the ground, and kept so by light logs of wood, and thus becomes fit for use.

Cedar slats were used as ribs to line and strengthen the bark interior of the canoe. Pieces of sharpened bone were used to make holes in the bark, and the roots of fir trees became the thread to hold the canoe together. While the men busied themselves with these tasks, the women chewed the gum of nearby fir trees until it became soft and pliable. With the aid of fire, this softened gum was applied to seal and tighten the seams of the canoe. The addition of gum on the seams worked well to prevent water from seeping in and destroying the provisions.

It required the combined labour of a man and woman for almost two weeks to construct an ordinary canoe. The results were well worth the effort: the finished product was light, swift, and had ample room for food and hunting or fishing equipment. In this craft the Indians made long journeys along Canada's lakes and rivers with remarkable ease and speed.

The size of the canoe varied according to the needs of its users; it might be constructed to carry as few as two or as many as fourteen people. Normally the canoe was paddled from a kneeling position, but an expert could stand up and pole in rapids. When rapids were too dangerous even for the experts, the canoe was paddled to the closest bank. If the water close to the bank was deep enough, the canoe was simply pushed or pulled along by a man on the bank. In some cases this was not possible and a land portage had to be made. One or two men would carry the canoe upside down over their shoulders—the light weight of the canoe was a real advantage—while the others carried the supplies and the wooden paddles. The length of the portage varied depending upon the size of the rapids. A portage also had to be made when land separated a river from a lake or stream. These portages were often as many as three or four miles long.

At night, when camp was made, the canoe was unloaded and tied to small wooden stakes in the ground—a necessary precaution because a sudden gust of wind might hurl the fragile craft into a nearby rock or tree. The ease with which it could be damaged was one of the major drawbacks of the canoe. A gentle bump against a sharp rock in the water usually spelled disaster. However, small mishaps resulting in minor damage were considered a normal part of the voyage. Supplies of fir roots, pliable gum, and a sharpened bone to use as a tool were always carried so that repairs could be made quickly on the spot.

Pulling a canoe past the rapids.
Why are they not shooting the rapids as in the previous picture?

A portage.
What advantages would a fibreglass canoe have over a wooden canoe when exploring the north today? What disadvantages would it have?

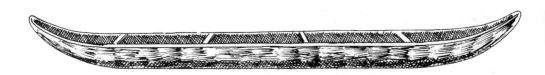

A dug-out canoe made out of a single large log.

Because of the constant danger that the canoe might capsize, the men wore little more than a loose-fitting robe that slipped off easily when necessary. Later, when the Europeans began to use the canoe, they often drowned because of the weight and constriction of their more elaborate garments.

The Iroquois, a league of tribes who lived in what is now New York State, did not have adequate supplies of large birch trees in their territory, and they were not nearly as skilled as the Algonkins at making canoes. The Iroquois canoe was constructed from a crudely hollowed pine tree with a point at the bow and the stern. These craft were so heavy, so easily waterlogged, and so impossible to portage that the Iroquois traded food and furs for the superior birch-bark canoes made by the Algonkins.

It is difficult to overestimate the importance of the canoe in the daily life of many of the eastern Indian tribes. It was used for both hunting and fishing: travelling by canoe made the journey to the hunting and fishing grounds much faster than otherwise would have been the case, and men were separated from their families only for short periods of time. The canoe allowed the various tribes to trade food, fur, and tobacco with their neighbours. The Hurons frequently traded corn and tobacco for fish, meat, and beaver pelts from the Algonkins. Even more important, however, is the fact that the Hurons, to name only one tribe, were forced to move their entire villages at least every ten years owing to their poor methods of farming, which exhausted the soil till the land could no longer produce a sufficient yield of corn. To move all the men, women, children, and supplies through the forests was not only a long and tiresome operation, it was also dangerous—it left the Hurons exposed to attack from other unfriendly tribes. The canoe, however, provided a faster, more comfortable, and usually a safer method of

10

Unloading in preparation for making a portage.
Explain the method used for carrying the packs.
What other ways are there of carrying heavy loads
without using machinery?

transportation than simply walking. Without the canoe the life of the Hurons, Algonkins, and to a lesser extent the Iroquois might have been very different.

But while the canoe was so important to the tribes of eastern Canada, it had little impact on the life of the tribes who lived on the Prairies. There the flat, treeless plains supplied neither the materials for making canoes nor the waterways on which to use them. The only way for the western tribes to travel was on foot—until they acquired horses from the south. Many of these tribes then became skilled horsemen and were able to use their wild horses to hunt the buffalo they had formerly pursued on foot.

While the life of the Indian was hard by today's standards, there was

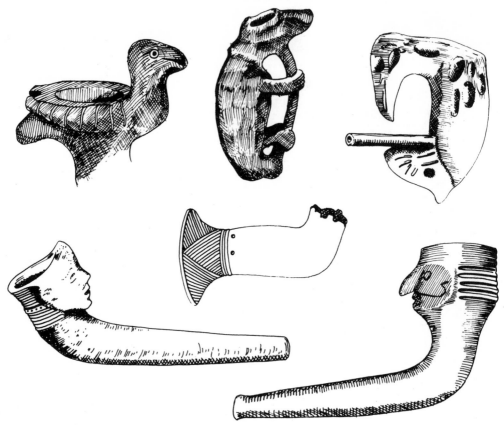

Huron-Iroquois and Algonkian pipes.

always a little time for games and celebrations. Lacrosse was considered not only an enjoyable pastime, but also an effective way of curing certain illnesses. For example, a sick Huron might dream that he was about to die unless lacrosse was played for his benefit. In response to his request, neighbouring villages might arrange to play against each other. Beaver robes, decorated bracelets, and even a man's scalp were often bet on the outcome. At the conclusion of the game the sick man might feel much better. Many of the players, however, lost almost everything they owned. This caused little bitterness—they would return to their villages naked and singing—because the Hurons believed that the spirits controlled the outcome of the game and that what was to be was to be.

To the Indians the spirits who lived on the earth, rivers, lakes, rocks, and sky controlled not only the outcome of games but the success of journeys, trading, hunting, and other matters. To ensure success in these undertakings, tobacco and prayers were offered up to the spirits. Often a man would throw some tobacco on the fire and pray to the spirits to protect his house from all harm. Whatever events followed these appeals to the spirits were accepted by the Indian with stoic resignation.

The significance of dreams in the life of North American Indians is well documented. According to Ojibway legend, the first knowledge of Europeans came through an old man's dream. 'Men of strange appearance,' he warned his friends, 'have come across the great water. Their skins are white like snow and on their faces long hair grows. These people have come across the great water in wonderfully large canoes which have great white wings like those of a giant bird. These men have long sharp knives, and they have long black tubes which they point at birds and animals. The tubes make a smoke that rises into the air just like the smoke from our pipes.'

When the Indians met the French, some important changes occurred among both groups. One group of people who took easily to the life and customs of the Indians were the coureurs de bois—'men of the woods'—who left the St Lawrence valley to travel by rivers and lakes to the north, the west, and the south in search of furs. The coureurs de bois were tough, daring men who were attracted by the lure of travel and the adventure of the fur trade. They became as skilled as the Indians themselves at managing the canoe. In fact many of these traders took to the Indian way of life completely, abandoning European clothes and customs in favour of Indian dress, wives, and friends. They were not at all daunted by the rigours of a wandering existence in the forests and on the plains of North America. In the words of Pierre Radisson, it was a life in which 'victuals are wanting, work whole nights and days, lie down on the bare ground, and not always happy.' After spending sometimes as long as eighteen months in distant parts, the coureurs de bois would return to the colony in the spring, their canoes loaded with valuable beaver furs. 'There arrived 20 or so canoes belonging to the coureurs de bois,' Baron de La Hontan wrote of their return to Montreal in 1685, 'being homeward bound from the Great Lakes and laden with beaver skins. The cargo of each canoe amounted to 40 packs, each of which weighs 50 pounds and will fetch 50 crowns at the farmers' office.'

After New France came under British control in 1763, the fur trade flourished more than ever. Scots, English, and American traders from Montreal—and their French-Canadian canoemen, called voyageurs—travelled farther into the northwest and even over the Rocky Mountains, which Alexander Mackenzie, who spent a large part of his life trading and exploring in Canada, crossed in 1793.

The canoes that left Lachine, near Montreal, each spring carried packages of 'woollen cloths of different kinds, milled blankets of different sizes; arms and ammunition; twists and carrot tobacco; linens; thread; lines and twine; common hardware; cutlery; kettles of brass and copper; handkerchiefs, hats, shoes; calicoes and printed cottons etc. etc.' for trading with the Indians. Each canoe also carried a sponge for bailing water, an axe, a towing line, a kettle, along with gum and bark for hasty repairs to the craft. Alexander Mackenzie wrote that a 'European, on seeing one of these slender vessels thus laden, heaped up and sunk with her gunwale within six inches of the water, would think his fate inevitable in such a boat, when he reflected on the nature of her voyage; but the Canadians [French-Canadian canoemen] are so expert that few accidents happen.'

The voyageurs who manned the canoes that travelled far into the interior of this unknown land were a brave and carefree lot who enjoyed the freedom and adventures of an exciting and dangerous life. When Simon Fraser made his heroic explorations down the treacherous Fraser River, he testified to the amazing skill of the voyageurs who manned the craft through dangerous and unknown waters.

It being absolutely impossible to carry the canoes by hand, yet sooner than abandon them, all hands embarked, as it were recklessly upon the mercy of the Stygian tide ... the die was cast, and the great difficulty consisted in keeping the canoes in the medium current, that is to say, clear of the precipice on one side, and of the gulphs formed by the waves on the other.

The canoes skimmed 'along like lightening; the crews, cool and determined, followed each other in awful silence. And when we arrived at the end we stood gazing on our narrow escape from perdition.'

A spring brigade leaving Montreal for the West.
What benefits were there in travelling in brigades?
These canoes would travel via the Ottawa River and
the Great Lakes to Fort William. Trace their
possible route on an atlas map and find out what
obstacles they might encounter.

To pass the time and keep the rhythm of the paddling brisk, the voyageurs sang folksongs with a lively tempo. Imagine a large canoe leaving Lachine with supplies for the inland posts. The day is bright and clear. The men are eager for adventure, eager to return to the freedom of the wilderness. The paddles feel light in their powerful hands. As Lachine fades into the distance someone begins a favourite tune—'En roulant ma boule' or 'A la claire fontaine'—and the others take it up.

Exaggeration and bravado were an essential part of their makeup. This is how one seventy-year-old voyageur recounted his life in the wilderness.

I was a light canoe man.... No portage was too long for me; all portages were alike.... Fifty songs a day were nothing to me. I could carry, walk, and sing with any man I ever saw.... No water, no weather, ever stopped the paddle or the song. I wanted for nothing; and I spent all my earnings in the enjoyment of pleasure. Yet were I young again, I should glory in commencing the same career again. I would spend another half century in the same fields of enjoyment. There is no life so happy as a voyageur's life; none so independent; no place where a man enjoys so much variety and freedom as in the Indian country.

It would be wrong, however, to think of the voyageur's life as primarily one of pleasure. Much of the time was spent in hard and sometimes monotonous labour. It was quite normal to paddle for eighteen hours a day. One particular crew managed to travel one hundred miles and make six portages in twenty-four hours. The voyageurs began the day's journey at two o'clock in the morning. There were halts for breakfast and for a midday meal. Every two hours they stopped for a smoke—distances were measured in *pipes*. By nine o'clock at night it was time to make camp, often in a swarm of mosquitoes, and to settle down for a few hours' sleep. Clearly this was no life for the weak or the lazy. The salary for such hardship and demanding physical labour was a mere eighteen pounds a year for paddlers. In addition, however, the men received food, clothing, and some type of lodging.

The Europeans living in the trading posts had to devote much of their time and energy to solving the problems of existence in an unfamiliar environment. The physical conditions were not easy; the

16

winters were always long and cold. Shelter and heat, food, clothing, travel, and defence occupied most of their time. The head of one trading post constantly complained that the chimneys 'are all so bad that we dare not light a fire in them and our Bricklayer so ignorant that he cannot repair them or at least not in sufficient time for the Winter Use. . . . I have been last winter under great anxiety of mind concerning them, the Men's House having once been on Fire & I dread the approaching winter with them in the same state.'

Much of the food and all of the goods stocked at the trading posts had to be supplied from Montreal. One trader grumbled about the inefficiency of the supply system. 'The large canoes always set off early in May,' he complained, 'and as the provisions they take with them are consumed by the time they reach Michilimacinac, they are necessitated to call there merely to take in an additional Supply, not only for themselves but also for the canoes intended for the Interior Country and the consumption of their servants. . . .'

A European fishing boat, about 1630, used on the St Lawrence.

The trading posts, and the fur trade itself, were still dependent on the canoe, and on the skills that the first Europeans had learned from the Indians and had continued to use for over one hundred years. The first French arrivals had benefited greatly from Indian skills. Since there were no roads, the Frenchmen could not travel on land as they had done in their home country by using wheeled carts, and so the canoe was as essential to the European for travel as to the Indian. The French relied on Indian knowledge of how to build, manage, and repair a birch-bark canoe, and on their skill in portaging. (Later they improved water travel by providing row boats, sail boats, and a crude knowledge of map-making.) The Indians' knowledge of how to travel through the forest on foot during the summer and on snowshoes during the winter was also essential to the French.

The snowshoe consisted of 'a light wooden frame of an oval shape, and is about forty inches long . . . and its weight is about two pounds. The whole surface within is formed of a network of thong, like that of a racket. . . . A small square aperture about the size of a man's hand is left in the net-work, into which the toes sink at every step, by which means the foot is prevented from slipping back.' The French experienced some difficulty in mastering snowshoes, and Indians often enjoyed the spectacle of a Frenchman flopping around on the snow like a helpless seal in a vain effort to right himself on the shoes after a fall. Despite the laughter of the Indians, the French struggled and finally succeeded in learning the skill of snowshoeing because they understood that it was essential for winter travel through the deep snow. And since the fur traders could not carry vast quantities of food with them, much of what they ate was suggested by the Indians.

For some years the Indians also prospered materially from their relationship with the Europeans. In return for the animal pelts they gave the fur traders, the Indians received merchandise that eased their everyday struggle for existence. The Frenchmen introduced iron cooking pots, knives, metal animal traps, fish hooks, hoes, and axes. The Indians expressed their gratitude by teaching the fur traders about the particular qualities and uses of various types of wood and the habits of the animals that roamed the forests. With the able assistance of their Indian guides, the Europeans rapidly expanded the fur trade and

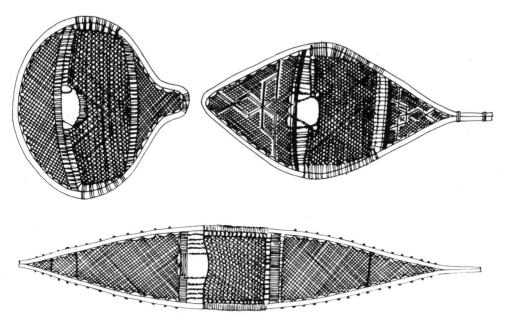

Ojibway, Montagnais, and western Cree snowshoes.

mapped the vast expanses of Canada. As a result, fertile land and great mineral wealth were discovered and utilized. Many highways in Ontario today still follow the routes of ancient Indian trails, and our railways often cross mountains through passes first discovered by the Indians.

Despite initial advantages, the long-term consequences of the arrival of the Europeans among the Indians were disastrous. Over time they became extremely dependent on the good will of the Europeans. Those Indians who gave up the bow and arrow for the musket gradually lost their native skills, and unless the Europeans continually replaced worn-out guns and provided ample shells, the Indians, who had long forgotten the old ways of the hunt, were doomed to starvation.

Other disadvantages were not as slow to manifest themselves. One was the unintentional introduction of certain diseases that had been unknown prior to the arrival of the Europeans. Mitchell Oman described the horrors of smallpox in one Indian village in 1781. 'None of us had the least idea of the desolation this dreadful disease had done, until we went up the bank to the camp and looked into the tents, in many of which they were all dead, and the stench was horrid; those that remained had pitched their tents about 200 yards from them and were too weak to move away entirely, which they soon intended to do; they were in such a state of despondence that they could hardly converse with us, a few of them had gained strength to hunt which kept them alive. From what we could learn three-fifths had died of the disease. They informed us that as far as they knew all the Indians were in the same dreadful state as themselves.'

Almost equally destructive was the introduction of alcohol into Indian culture. 'They do not call it drinking,' wrote one fur trader, 'unless they become drunk, and do not feel they have been drinking unless they fight and are hurt.' The Indian women lived in constant fear of alcohol and often gathered their children and hid in the woods when a fresh keg of liquor was brought from the trading post. Whisky and brandy not only helped to destroy the self-respect of the Indians but also made them slaves of the trading post.

More and more furs were demanded at the trading posts in return for liquor, guns, and ammunition. To meet the demand the Indians had begun by trapping these animals in their own territory; and then, when the supply was depleted, in areas occupied by their neighbours. Warfare frequently resulted. There was a gradual weakening of the strong spirit of community that had previously existed among the various tribes as trapping took the men farther away from the villages for longer and longer periods. The old ways and ancient customs were ridiculed by the so-called civilized Europeans until the Indian lost respect both for himself and for his heritage. Perhaps it was inevitable that Indian culture would be forced to change under the onslaught of European ways. It is certain, though, that greater tolerance and understanding would have eased the transition for the Canadian Indian.

2 Sleighs and Rafts

The excitement and romance of the lives of the early fur traders and explorers often obscure the contribution made by those who came to till the fields of New France. One of the first families to do so was that of Louis Hébert. Life in the little settlement at Québec was not easy, but the Héberts were not strangers to hardship: they had attempted once before to settle in Acadia, but had been forced to return to France when the settlement was destroyed in a raid in 1613. In 1617 Hébert, his wife, and three children were prepared to try once again. And so they set sail for Québec.

The ocean voyage to New France was both dangerous and extremely uncomfortable. Father Paul Le Jeune, for example, left·France on April 18, 1632 for the colony. After some weeks at sea, the ship 'was left to the will of the billows and waves, which bore it at times upon mountains of water. . . . Every moment we feared lest they should snap our masts, or that the ship would spring a leak; and, in fact, there was a leak, which would . . . have sunk us if it had been lower down.' The passengers 'ate nothing but salted food, and there was no fresh water on our vessel. The size of our cabins was such that we could not stand upright, kneel or sit down; and what is worse, during the rain, the water fell at times upon our face.' Two months and eighteen days later the

A sailing ship of about 1658.
Why would the journey from France to Québec take so long in this ship?
Locate a map of prevailing winds and trace a likely course for the ship across the Atlantic.
Estimate the distance travelled, and determine the approximate speed of the ship Father Le Jeune travelled in. Compare its speed with that of a modern passenger liner today.

good Father reached Québec. His experiences were common enough to frighten away many prospective settlers.

The European population of New France took a long while to grow. Gabriel Sagard, a missionary who came to Québec in 1623, wrote that the settlement was 'almost uninhabited and uncultivated, and this through the negligence and lack of interest of the merchants . . . who have been satisfied to get furs and profit out of it without having been willing to make any outlay for cultivation, settlement, or the progress of the country.' By 1627 there were only five families of workmen who could truly be called settlers. Only seven acres were under cultivation. The population was only 279 in 1640, 675 in 1650, 3,035 in 1663. The trading companies that controlled the fur trade tended to discourage colonists because they feared that the growth of settlement would be harmful to their business interests. The beaver and other small fur-bearing animals would move farther and farther away; the Indians would also move and would be reluctant to trade as the French population increased. The companies refused to supply equipment for the settlers to work with—they did not want valuable cargo space in the ships taken up with ploughs and animals. They required blankets, pots, knives, and rifles that they could trade with the Indians for the valuable furs. Only in 1628 was there a plough and an ox to draw it.

Cut off from the comparative comforts and security of France, the newcomers were forced to battle the climate as well as the Iroquois. News of home, and the essential supplies of food and ammunition, came to the colony only once a year with the ships, and those flimsy lifelines, often all that stood between the settlers and starvation, were subject to the destruction wrought by European wars and inclement weather. After passing through famine conditions for many months, one disgusted Frenchman wrote to relatives in France that the situation had been so grim that the people had been forced to eat 'buds of trees, potatoes and other foods never intended to be used as food for human beings.'

One reason there were not more people in New France was seen to be a shortage of women. To remedy this situation the King of France arranged to send eligible young women and widows to his colony. 'Ninety two girls have come from France this year,' wrote Marie de l'Incarnation in 1667, 'who are married (for the most part) to soldiers or labourers, who are given a habitation and food for eight months so that they can clear fields to maintain themselves.'

From this experience the Intendant of New France recognized that certain women were more suited than others to the rigours of life in the colony. He recommended to the King that girls sent to New France 'should not be disagreeable by nature ... and should not be bad looking. They should be healthy and strong for work in the country or at least should have some training in handicrafts.'

The success of this policy was reported by Jean Talon, Intendant of the colony in 1671. Between six and seven hundred children had been born in the colony that year. 'There is some reason to believe,' he wrote, 'that, without any further female immigration, the country will see more than one hundred marriages next year. I consider it unnecessary to send girls next year; the better to give the habitants a chance to marry their own girls to soldiers desirous of settling.'

Not all those who lived in the colony became farmers. In fact not enough men chose this pursuit. There were administrators, military officers, and merchants who did not intend to stay longer than it took

A Habitant farm.
What was the building to the left of the house used for?
Explain why owning a horse was important to a farmer in New France.

to make their fortunes. Others were more interested in using skills they had learned in France. Jean Talon reported that 'at the present time I have enough products from Canada to clothe me from head to foot. . . . And I hope that in a short time the country will want nothing from Old France save a few necessities.' Subsidies to local industries, the introduction of an apprenticeship system, and the importation of skilled workers from France broadened the economic base of the colony.

And there were the coureurs de bois. Even though furs were of prime importance to the economy, the lure of the fur trade became a grave problem. Rural life lacked variety and many found life in the colony too confining. Too many sons of settlers were eager to leave the St Lawrence to become coureurs de bois. All the efforts of both Church and government to stop this state of affairs proved to be in vain: every year more men took to the woods. Often they left behind a wife and

French-Canadian
farmers, early
nineteenth century.

family; some farms were abandoned altogether. At times it seemed as if the fur trade would destroy the settlement itself.

Apart from the monotony of rural life, another factor contributing to the lure of the fur trade may have been the difficulties faced by the early farmer or habitant. The land had to be cleared of trees and ploughed in preparation for the first crops. Since at first there were no work animals (and of course no machines), everything had to be done by hand.

The work of the farm generally followed the seasons. Springtime was for planting, late summer and fall were devoted to harvesting, storing, and sometimes selling surplus produce. Jean-Baptiste d'Aleyrac, an officer stationed in New France in the middle of the eighteenth century, was intrigued by the fact that the people spent much of the late summer and fall preparing for the long winter. 'They provide themselves with everything for the winter while the summer is still with us,' he wrote. 'They kill everything they require for the period from the end of November until the end of April, when the snow has gone and the thaw has come. They stock up on meat,' he continued, 'as if they would eat it at a single meal and they put it in a storehouse where it freezes and is thus preserved. When they want to eat it they thaw it over a stove, and thus prepare it as if it came straight from the butcher; for by this time the meat is still as fresh and good as when it was killed.'

Aside from preparing for winter, the men and boys were also busy caring for the livestock, fishing, and repairing the house and other buildings. During the winter, when the land was covered by a thick blanket of snow, the men spent their days making furniture or carving wooden figures, as well as hunting, fishing, and caring for the livestock.

Every day, regardless of the season, there were important tasks to be performed. Milk from the family cow, for those who were lucky enough to have such a beast, was laboriously churned into butter that was preserved for festive occasions or for the unexpected arrival of visitors. Water for drinking and cooking had to be fetched either from the river or from a hand-dug well close to the house. In the winter, blocks of ice were carried to the house and melted for the family's use. It is easy to imagine how awkward it must have been to keep the family clean, and how time-consuming such everyday chores as washing clothes were for the habitant family. Each day wood had to be chopped for the fireplace. In winter a great deal of wood was needed to keep the family warm during the long, cold nights. In the summer smaller quantities were needed, just for cooking. Of necessity all work stopped with the setting of the sun. The dim light given out by the candles was not sufficient to work by, and once the evening meal had been eaten the family was ready to retire for the night.

The colonist's home was usually built of logs, smoothed on the outside and then whitewashed to give a clean appearance. The house was built low with a very steep roof that prevented the winter snows from accumulating and, perhaps, crushing the entire structure with its weight. The huge fireplace was an important part of the house and had to be built with special care and attention. For the most part the fireplace was constructed with deep pocket-like ovens on each side of

A wooden house with an elevated gallery in Québec.

the stone hearth. Fires were built in these small ovens. When the stone became white hot, the ashes from the fire were swept out and bread or cakes, which had been placed in a small black iron kettle, were put into the ovens to bake. Great pride was taken in the quality of the baked goods thus produced.

The risk of fire was constant and everyone had to exercise caution when cooking or adding fuel to the fireplace. Some early settlers decided to build stone houses like those in France and thus eliminate the serious threat of fire that faced those who lived in wooden dwellings. These first stone homes, however, were not well suited to the climate of Canada. The stone kept the houses very cold during the winter months, and the mortar that held the stones in place chipped and cracked in the low winter temperatures. To make matters worse, the foundations were quickly cracked and ruined by the shifting frosts. Later houses were built on a stone foundation covered with straw and earth to protect it from the cold. With their steep, high-pitched roofs and their two-feet-thick whitewashed walls lined on the inside with wooden laths covered with plaster, some of these houses have stood for two centuries and can be seen today.

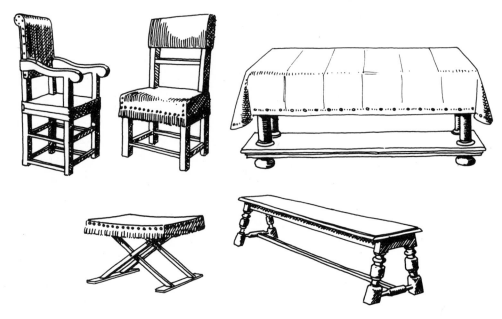

French furniture of the early seventeenth century,
brought to New France for the houses of the
well-to-do.

The interior of the colonist's home boasted few if any luxuries. The main room doubled as a kitchen and a bedroom. At one end of the room stood a large canopied bed. Beds or cradles for the children stood nearby. The rest of the furniture consisted of wooden chairs, a table, a spinning wheel, and a loom. The women took great pains to make their homes as attractive as possible, and they quickly developed a knack for making whatever was needed out of anything that was available. The colourful handwoven rugs that both covered the timber floors and added warmth to their homes were made from scraps of worn-out clothing. Fur skins from bears and other animals were used as bed coverings during the winter. One visitor to the colony commented that the typical home was 'a little house with verandahs all round, few windows and few fancies; everything was done with an air of humble comfort.'

The women of New France became expert at candle- and soap-making. To make soap they first burned such hardwoods as oak, beech, and maple in the fireplace. The ashes were then carefully swept into an old iron or tin container. Once the ashes cooled they were removed to a wooden barrel and two quarts of good lime were added. The contents of the barrel were pounded and water was added to keep the mixture moist. The barrel was then left to sit until the mixture separated itself into lye, which was used for making soap, and sediment, which was thrown away. Several pounds of grease from the entrails of pigs and other animals were then added to the lye. This new mixture was transferred to a metal pot and boiled until it reached the right consistency. Then it was allowed to cool slightly before being transferred to a wooden keg in which the soap eventually hardened.

The women of New France showed their ingenuity in other ways too. On those special occasions when visitors were expected or visits were made to neighbours, the women could only dress in the rough woollen clothes they had made themselves. There were no expensive cosmetics, but it soon became common knowledge that beet roots were an ideal substitute. Many of the women of New France rouged their cheeks with beet juice on social occasions.

For all their toil, the habitants were a cheerful people. They were said to have a very good opinion of themselves, as well they might, for they were independent, self-sufficient, and contented. They needed little besides the essentials of life and these they provided for themselves, growing their own food and making all their clothes.

Much of the social activity of these people naturally centred on their church. As information could only be passed from one person to another by letters or orally, the church was one of the most important meeting places for the French settlers. Aside from providing a time and place for the exchange of information, the church was also a source of help to those in material as well as spiritual distress. Often the parish priest or curé sought help from the members of his congregation for a particular family in need. Sometimes donations of bread, vegetables, or meat were offered; others gave a little of their time to planting or harvesting for the family.

Some of the most important festivities in the colony revolved around

Left: Church at Cap-de-la-Madeleine, built about
1717.
Right: Notre Dame de Bon-Secours, Montreal, as it
appeared in 1880.

the church. Christmas and the all-important Jour Gras were directly
related to the spiritual tenets of Catholicism. The Jour Gras, which was
held before the long period of fasting during Lent began, was an
especially festive occasion. In New France the day was marked by a
respite from work, visits to neighbours, and a great dinner with as many
luxuries as the family could afford.

Before there were roads, the St Lawrence and other rivers were the
primary highways. Even when a rough road was built between Montreal
and Québec in 1734, the fastest and most comfortable way to travel
downriver was still by water.

The canoe was the chief means of transportation for the first men and
women who came to Canada to settle rather than to trade in furs. Ira
Honeywell, a young settler near the present location of Ottawa, often
travelled alone to Montreal for such supplies as flour and salt and sugar,
which were essential for the long winter months. Early each fall this

30

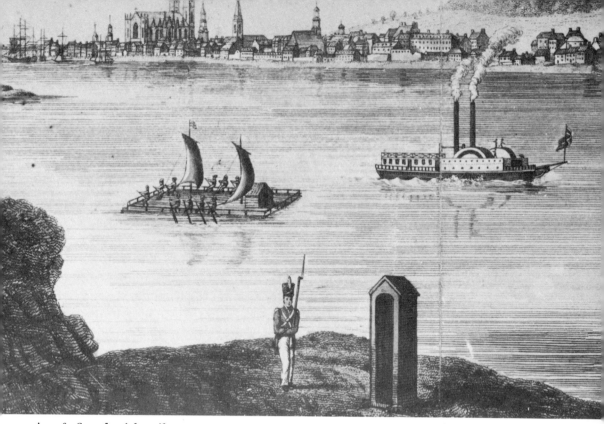

A raft fitted with sails.
Why are both sails and oars being used on the raft?

brave fellow set out by canoe to face the perils of the long journey.
Imagine his feelings as he paddled down the Ottawa River with only
the sound of the paddle splashing the cold, clear water and the twitter-
ing of birds to break the silence. Occasionally a moose or a deer might
be spotted drinking or wading near the river banks. At night the sky
was his roof. To the early settlers the Canadian forest was dangerous,
and so Ira Honeywell probably slept lightly, listening for the sharp
cracking of twigs that would signal the presence of unwanted visitors.

In addition to the canoe, the cajeu was an important form of water
transportation because it allowed the farmer to carry heavy, bulky goods
along the waterways of New France. The cajeu was a form of raft made
out of pieces of wood that were solidly bound together with whatever
material happened to be at hand. Although this raft was crudely
constructed, it was easily fitted with sails when the winds were high.
Since the cajeux were too heavy to be carried around rapids and other

31

obstacles, they were simply abandoned on the bank, and travellers going in the opposite direction were free to make use of them.

The importance of the rivers extended even beyond their use as major arteries for travel. The St Lawrence provided water for the early settlers, their livestock, and their crops. Fish from the river assisted the farmer in varying or supplementing the family diet. It is not surprising, then, that the importance of land with river frontage was not lost on prospective farmers. Each settler insisted that his parcel of land must border on the St Lawrence.

As agricultural settlement was primarily confined to the banks of the St Lawrence during the seventeenth century, the pioneers of New France were spared some of the loneliness and isolation that later English 'backwoods' settlers would face. From spring through fall the canoe provided a convenient method of getting from one neighbour to another. During the winter months, when work in the fields came to a halt and the frozen river was not open to travel by canoe, the homemade sleigh or carriole came into its own. By the early eighteenth century most families were able to afford a horse and sleigh.

The runners of the sleigh were high and thin to allow the vehicle to cut more easily through the snow. The body of the sleigh was very low, and as the horse pulled the sleigh over the ice and snow at what seemed breakneck speeds, the occupants often wondered if they were going to crash. Since the sleigh had no roof, the wind and blowing snow might dampen the enthusiasm of the less hearty. Most families, however, braced themselves against the cold by dressing in their warmest home-spun garments, complete with woollen toque to protect their ears. A thick blanket or bearskin was also carried as a further defence against the cold. Heated logs were sometimes placed on the floor of the sleigh to prevent frozen toes and feet. The rare pleasure of a sleighing party was one of the bright spots of winter. Every family eagerly awaited the special day when friends and neighbours would join together for an outing in a sleigh.

The sleigh was also the preferred form of winter transportation among the officers stationed in New France. Their sleighs were some-what more elaborate, with soft upholstered seats and gay decorations. Such was the popularity of the sleigh that the Governor issued regula-

A variety of sleighs still in use in Montreal in 1830.
*What are the advantages and disadvantages of the
various kinds of sleighs?*

An officer in his sleigh.
Why were military men stationed in New France?

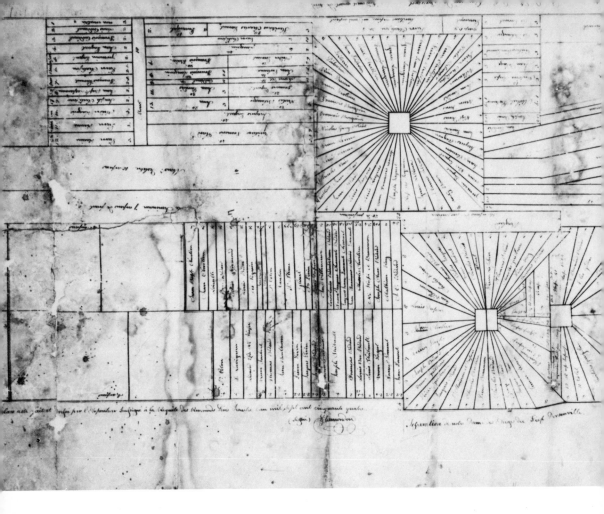

tions dealing with the traffic situation that developed each Sunday in Québec after Mass, In 1716 Canada's first traffic laws were posted on the door of every church so that all might be informed of the regulations as quickly as possible.

We forbid all persons, drivers of carrioles as well as those on horseback, to allow trotting or galloping while the congregation leaves the church, until they are ten arpents from the church; afterwards they may give their horses their heads provided there is no one ahead of them. . . .

Not everyone, however, was a sleighing enthusiast. It was necessary 'to retain fast hold of the side' of the sleigh, and 'the bumps and jerks were such as cannot be readily imagined.' One person complained that 'nothing could be worse than the motion of a sleigh on a rough road. . . .

34

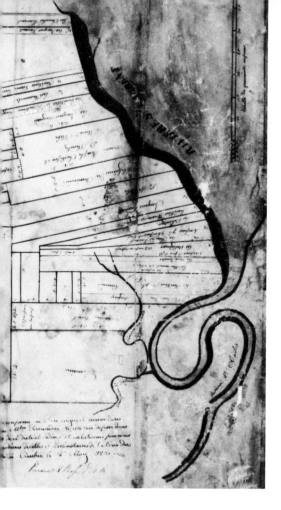

Map of Notre-Dame-des-Anges, Québec, 1754.
Why did the shape of the lots change away from the river?

The jolts inflicted by lumps of hard snow and other obstacles may be compared to the blows of a short chopping sea upon a boat making headway against wind and tide.' And unsafe ice swallowed the horse and sleigh of more than one driver.

For those who disliked the sleigh, there were sleds drawn by dogs on the ice or frozen snow of the river. If that did not please, skates or snowshoes could be used to get around on foot. The early Governor of Québec often hired skaters to deliver important messages to officials in Montreal and Trois-Rivières. A story is told of one messenger who skated from Montreal to Québec, a distance of one hundred and eighty miles, in a mere eighteen hours. Upon his arrival in Québec the messenger dropped dead without disclosing the news from Montreal.

In August 1749 Peter Kalm, a professor of natural history who was

Québec, around 1785.
What is being harvested at the left of the picture?
What would indicate that this farm is more
prosperous than the one in the picture on page 24?

visiting from Sweden, travelled from Montreal to Québec by boat and
described a river view of a countryside that was dotted with houses,
windmills, and churches. 'The prospect is exceedingly beautiful when
the river flows on for several miles in a straight line,' he wrote, 'because
it then shortens the distances between the houses and makes them form
a continuous village.' But when waterfront lots were no longer readily
available, inland settlement began. Since these later farms were not
adjacent to the water, a new means of transportation had to be devised.
And so the first dirt roads came to be built in the colony.

But roads did not eliminate the perils of winter transportation. There
was the cold, so bitter that unprotected ears and fingers were likely to
freeze. The other danger, and perhaps the one most feared, was the
likelihood of losing one's way in a snowstorm and freezing to death as a
consequence. To avoid this the following order was issued in 1727 to
all settlers:

*It is therefore necessary to order the settlers ... whose homesteads
are sited on the larger roads, to mark them ... in such a way that
travellers are in no danger of losing their way.*

Roads were naturally built in the towns earlier than in the countryside, and as a result the towns became the centres of more sophisticated

36

Crossing the ice by boat.
Why was this hazardous way of crossing the river used?

forms of amusement than were available to the habitant. One such town was Québec, the seat of government. It spilled down a cliff at a narrowing of the river. It was like a small city of France. In its Upper Town, on top of the cliff, were the Governor's residence, the Château St Louis, several churches, chapels, a hospital, spacious buildings, squares, and rough, twisted streets. In Lower Town were shops and warehouses, the stone houses of the merchants and the more modest homes of the artisans, clerks, and labourers. Québec had an aristocratic society that moved around the court of the Governor. It was greatly enjoyed by the government officials, landowners of the region, and army officers and their wives. The people of Québec partied continually. In summer they went on carriage and canoe rides; in winter sleighing, tobogganing, skating, dancing, cards, and billiards occupied their leisure time. 'There is nobody rich here,' wrote Father Charlevoix, 'and 'tis pity, for they love to live generously and no one thinks of laying up riches. They keep good tables if their fortunes will afford it, as well as dress handsomely; if not, they retrench the expense of their table to bestow it on dress.'

The people of Québec used the canoe to transport mail, freight, and passengers across the St Lawrence to Pointe Lévis. As late as February 1839 sixteen passengers perished when a canoe was upset among pieces of floating ice while making the crossing from Pointe Lévis to Québec. One thoroughly frightened traveller described his mid-winter trip across the St Lawrence in the following way:

We got into the canoe upon the wharf, stretched ourselves at the bottom thereof, were muffled up to our eyes in furs, and as our friends crowded round the long narrow receptacle I felt excessively as if I was already in my coffin, and was only waiting to be let down.

The boatmen are fine muscular men, in shaggy beards and coats, who sing the old songs of the Canadian voyageurs. . . .

We edge our way through the narrow lanes of water between the ice-fields, following a devious course, sometimes breaking through a thin crust of ice, until our progress is altogether arrested; then the voyageurs jump out, and pull the canoe upon the ice . . . and rattle us over the jagged surface to the flow until we reach open water, when we are again launched, and at last, to our great gratification, find ourselves pulled up under the steep bank at Pointe Lévis.

The river still played a dominant part in the life of even the sophisticated Québécois, and afforded dangers and difficulties as well as pleasures.

3 Horses and Coaches

Those men and women who came to Canada from the United States during and after the War of Independence are known as the United Empire Loyalists. More often than not they came from comfortable homes and were strangers to the intense hardship and loneliness that invariably accompanied the pioneer conditions they were to meet with in Upper Canada, or what is now known as Ontario.

They came in rude wooden carts pulled slowly by heavy oxen, or they walked. All their belongings came with them in wooden trunks and crates. Anything too large to carry was either left behind or sold, depending on the haste with which these people left their homes.

Jane Spring, a young girl of twelve, made the journey with her parents from New York to the Niagara peninsula in three gruelling weeks. Jane described part of the trip in a letter written to her sister, who had remained in the United States with her husband.

We drove our ox carts, two of them, and brought our sheep and cattle. The morning after our first stop, Father milked the cows and put the sweet milk in the stone churn. By night the milk was churned into butter, for the Indian trails that we followed were so rough and we had the sweet buttermilk for our supper.... We got to a place called Hamilton where only one man by that name lived in a log cabin under the mountain, in the midst of forest.

Encampment of the Loyalists on the banks of the St Lawrence, 1784.
Find out why the United Empire Loyalists left the United States. Do you know of any other groups of people who left their country recently for political reasons?

The roads were invariably poor; even the best ones were little more than slightly improved Indian trails. Roadways were so narrow that the trees met overhead and prevented any sunlight from striking the ground. During the spring and fall these trails were for the most part impassable, for rain could transform them into raging torrents of mud and debris. 'Holes masked by mud,' lamented one weary traveller, 'were of constant occurrence—into these our vehicle plunged with a crash.' These mud-filled holes tipped and broke the axle of more than one unsuspecting driver's cart.

Fallen trees and unmoveable tree stumps were further obstacles. There were few bridges to speak of, and so the chilly creeks and streams that criss-crossed the traveller's path had to be traversed on foot by those who did not have carts. One early settler found himself in an awkward situation when he had to ford the Thames River. 'In the middle it pleased the oxen to stop, and as we were all on the waggon, they being quite out of our reach.' The more the driver shouted 'Haw, Haw, then!' the more the tired beasts appeared indifferent. 'At length, however, they were "graciously pleased" to tug us up the bank.'

Others, perhaps more fortunate, made their way from the United

States to the British colonies on crowded ships that sailed along the eastern seaboard. Some stayed in Nova Scotia and New Brunswick while others made their way to the province of Québec. The officials there were faced with the task of assigning property to these new settlers. The head of each household was given a slip of paper that described the general location of his land. With this safely tucked away, the settlers set out for their destination in wooden vessels that varied in size and were known as bateaux. The bateau was a flat-bottomed craft, usually constructed of the finest available white oak. Four or five wooden slats were laid sideways across the boat as seats to provide a more comfortable ride for the crew, who rowed or poled the craft along the St Lawrence. When the wind was high, large square sails were hoisted to give the bateau more speed. While the bateau was very difficult to capsize and fairly easy to row in calm waters, the journey to Upper Canada was still a long and uncomfortable one.

In the first place the bateau offered no protection from the hot rays of the summer sun or from unexpected showers. The settlers slept night after night on the shore, where they were equally at the mercy of the weather and were liable to be awakened by the damp morning dew.

41

The Concord coach.

There were no wayside inns in those days where travellers could stay overnight.

On cool, sunny days the trip was almost pleasant, despite the fact that the bateau was usually overcrowded with as many as five or six families and all their belongings. But the pleasures of the trip were few. At the approach of rapids or strong currents a sharp command reminded all aboard that they must disembark at once. Each passenger had to jump into the chilly water and be prepared to assist the crew in hauling the bateau past whatever obstacle they had encountered. Everyone then climbed back in, dripping wet, and the journey continued.

The Loyalists who travelled to the Upper St Lawrence and the shores of Lake Ontario were not entirely without resources. Every two families were given a whip saw and a crosscut saw. A valuable set of small tools was shared among every five families. Hoes, spades, and seeds were given to everyone as long as supplies held out. A few very fortunate families were supplied with cattle. Everyone was also given provisions of food for at least the first year.

When the Loyalists reached the general area in which their land was located, a host of problems awaited them. Often they had to wait for the surveyor to complete his work of dividing the land up into lots. Then a draw was held to determine who was to receive each parcel of land. Once the exact location was assigned, the head of the household was then faced with the task of getting to his particular piece of property. There were no roads in most of these areas; often there was not even an adequate map to follow. In more than one case it was difficult, if not impossible, to establish precise boundaries.

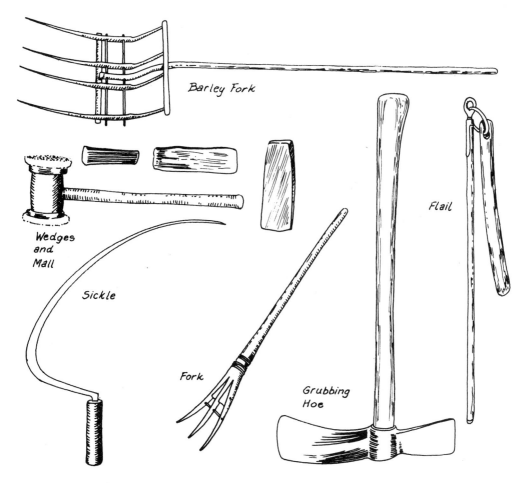

Farm tools.

Once the Loyalist family reached their land they were probably shocked. How could this wild forest be transformed into a productive farm? The first tasks to be undertaken were the clearing of the land and the construction of a shelter. While the mother began to organize the family's belongings and store the provisions out of the reach of young children or wild animals, the men and older boys began to clear the land with hand axes. Some logs were set aside to build a shanty to house the family over the winter. The others, along with the brush and undergrowth, were dragged or rolled into huge piles and set ablaze. More often than not these fires spread to the adjacent forest. If the weather had been particularly dry, a fire might destroy acres of beautiful woods, as one account shows.

If the weather is very dry, and a brisk wind blowing, the work of destruction proceeds with astonishing rapidity: sometimes the fire will communicate with the forest and run over many hundreds of acres. This is not considered favorable for clearing, as it destroys the under-brush and light timbers, which are almost indispensable for ensuring a good burning. It is however a magnificent sight to see the blazing trees and watch the awful progress of the conflagration, as it hurries onward, consuming all before it, or leaving such scorching mementos as have blasted the forest growth for years ...

This initial clearing and burning process was both difficult and slow, and even when it was completed the fields were still spotted with the huge stumps of the felled trees. Beech, oak, maple, and elm stumps usually decayed if they were left for about ten years. The hardy pine stumps were a different matter. The decaying process was very much slower and their final removal required more burning or the aid of oxen to extract them from the land. Such stumps when removed were used to mark boundary lines and can still be seen in some rural areas today.

Once a little land had been cleared, the settler sowed his first crop. At the same time as the land was being cleared, the settler had to devote his efforts to constructing some sort of shelter. The first home was usually a shanty, a temporary structure designed to meet the immediate needs of the family. Of necessity it was quite small—about ten feet by eight feet and not more than six feet high. The shanty usually had no windows, but there was no lack of fresh air because there were always gaps between the logs; in winter, of course, these gaps allowed unwanted ventilation. The doorway was cut after all the logs had been notched and fitted into place. For a while at least a blanket or rug was used as a door covering. By no means warm or dry, these shanties did offer some protection from the elements, though one woman complained that 'The shanty to which we went had a bark roof and this roof leaked so badly that when it rained my husband had to hold an umbrella over us.'

Susanna Moodie, who came to Upper Canada in 1832, found condi-

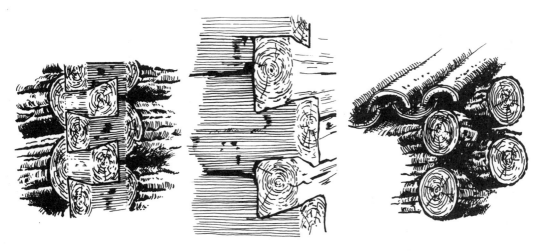

Left: Squared logs with bark left on the outside.
Centre: Squared-log construction.
Right: Round-log construction, with a roof of basswood bark.

tions much the same as those faced by the Loyalists forty or fifty years earlier. Although she was a natural complainer, Mrs Moodie probably did not exaggerate when she described co-operative shanty building and its results. 'They talk of log houses to be raised in a single day by the generous exertions of friends and neighbours,' she wrote, 'but they never ventured upon a picture of the disgusting scenes of riot and debauchery exhibited during the raising, or upon a description of the dwellings when raised—dens of dirt and misery, which would, in many instances, be shamed by an English pig sty.' Mrs Moodie's sister, Mrs Traill, who came to Canada in the same year complained of the terrible cold that shanty-dwellers endured. 'The sensation of cold in the early morning,' she wrote, 'is very painful, producing an involuntary shuddering and an almost convulsive feeling in the chest. Our breaths were congealed in hoar-frost on the sheets and blankets. Everything we touched of metal seemed to freeze our fingers.'

It is not surprising, then, that the Loyalists and later settlers built better homes as soon as they were able and turned the shanties over to the cows or pigs, if they had any. This second home was always larger than the shanty and might have a small upstairs loft for use as a sleeping

45

Bush farm near Chatham about 1838.
Is this a shanty or the second home of a settler?

chamber. Each tree trunk used in building it was squared by means of an axe or saw; little notches were made at each end so that the logs would fit neatly together. The gaps between the logs were filled with moss or wooden wedges and clay. The roof was often constructed from cedar logs that were halved, though a more prosperous settler might use handmade shingles. The floor was usually covered with rough planks. Doors and window openings were cut after the walls had been raised, as in a shanty. Very few enjoyed the luxury of glass windows; most people simply had openings with cloth or paper coverings.

Not a single nail was used in building either the shanty or the second home, but the ingenuity of these pioneers enabled them to build reasonably solid homes without nails. The major problem was that their dwellings had no basements. As a result heavy frosts and the

The interior of a house in Fenelon Falls about 1840.
What indications are there that this might be
considered a luxurious dwelling?

process of rotting shifted the house in one or more places, causing
uneven floors and a general weakening of the entire structure.

The fireplace was the central feature of the house because it was the
only source of heat. It also served as an oven. Made of stone or a
mixture of stones, logs, and clay, it was sometimes as wide as eight feet.
Obviously the fireplace was useless without a fire. Matches were not
invented until 1829 and were not in common use until many years
later. Once a fire had been started, every effort was made to keep it
alight, and woe to the young boy or girl who was left to watch the fire
and let it go out! It might be necessary to make a hasty trip through the
forest to the nearest neighbour five miles or more away to get a burning
ember from which a new fire could be lighted. Such errands were far
from pleasant when the cry of wolves could be heard in the distance.

Another room in the same house.
Think of a use for all the implements hanging on the wall.

The threat of wolves was very real in the minds of the early settlers. Jane Spring wrote of one experience in September 1794.

I think the most exciting time last year was one evening when Father and William were away . . . the cattle were in a habit of going a mile or two back into the forest. I set out following an Indian trail. Wolves were plentiful and I was nervous, but I took a heavy club with me . . . when almost to the cattle, a wolf near the trail set up a howl and soon a pack of wolves appeared . . . a thought entered my head and as the old cow with the bell passed, I grabbed her tail and hung on . . . I depended on that cow to bring me out to the clearing . . . I took steps ten feet long . . . when Father and William saw the trouble I was in, they grabbed their guns and managed to get two or three . . .

There was a general shortage of cattle in pioneer communities at this time and the Spring family was fortunate to have some of its own. To meet the need for cattle among the pioneers, James Lickley of Peterborough came up with a rather ingenious scheme. He decided to rent a cow and calf to nearby residents for a period of three years. The original cow and calf were returned to Lickley with a flat fee at the end of the rental period, while any additional offspring were the property of the settler. So precious were cattle at this time that many settlers tied their livestock to the door of their shanty at night to protect the animals from wolves or would-be thieves.

Travel was so difficult during the early days of settlement that the pioneers had to supply themselves with all the basic needs. Like the settlers in New France over a hundred years earlier, these people made everything, from clothing to candles, at home. Jane Spring's mother, like most pioneer women, spun 'the wool into yarn and makes us all warm socks, mittens and cloth.' Goldenrod was boiled to make a yellow dye for the wool. Grey came from the bark of the maple tree, while a brownish hue could be made by boiling the bark of the butternut tree. A much-admired pale-fawn shade was obtained by boiling the outer skins of onions. Making candles was a relatively simple though time-consuming task. Fat from animals was saved and then cut into small pieces and placed in a clean pot with a little water. When the fat was boiling hot it was put through a flannel strainer into a pot or tin dish. A length of wick was placed in a candle mould into which the tallow (boiled fat) was poured. The mould was allowed to cool and then more

A mould for making candles.

hot tallow was poured in because there was a tendency for the tallow to shrink in size. Once the tallow had cooled in the mould it was removed. The finished candles were kept in a cool dry place, carefully covered lest the mice help themselves.

One thing that the Loyalists and later settlers really missed was a nearby mill to grind their wheat into fine white flour for bread and cakes. Early settlers often described long difficult journeys by canoe or bateau to obtain this highly valued product. Roger Bates, who settled in Durham County near Bowmanville in 1793, sometimes made a five-to-six-week trip by bateau to Kingston to have his wheat ground into flour. Because of the lineups at the mill he often had to wait several days for his turn. Jane's family ground their wheat at home, but the results were barely satisfactory. Like mill flour, this home-ground product was used for bread that was baked in iron kettles over the fireplace. Doughnuts were also made from home-ground flour and cooked in an iron basin filled with bear's grease. Bear's grease was particularly useful because it evaporated very slowly and could be used over and over again. The other staples of the pioneer diet were salted pork, fish, potatoes, and corn.

Salt was one necessity of life that the pioneers could not produce on their own. The difficulty involved in procuring enough salt for a family's needs is well illustrated by the misadventures of one early settler. 'In the winter of 1813,' he wrote, 'I went to Long Point and paid $6 for 28 pounds, a neighbour offering to take it home in his sleigh. He stayed overnight on the road, but left his load exposed, so that a cow destroyed the salt, killed herself and caused me to return to replace the loss. This necessitated two hundred miles of travel on foot and $12 in cash, to realize 28 pounds of salt.'

In the summer the settlers supplemented their diet with wild raspberries, blackberries, blueberries, gooseberries, and cranberries. Hemlock 'tea' and Indian corn 'coffee' were used as substitutes for the real thing. Although turkey, ducks, pigeons, deer, and rabbits were plentiful, the high cost of ammunition often curtailed hunting. Pigeon meat was considered a delicacy and the feathers were used for stuffing pillows and quilts.

Money for salt and ammunition was often made from the vast

A corduroy road.
Would walking have been easy on roads like these?
How did corduroy roads assist wagons in crossing
wet areas?

forests that blanketed the settler's land. Sometimes he burned the maple and elm trees into fine ashes that were then leached. The resulting lye was boiled down in great iron kettles to make salts. These salts were then packed and taken directly to Toronto, Montreal, or Québec where they were further processed into potash—one of the essential ingredients for making soap. In Nova Scotia and especially New Brunswick cash income could be made by selling the timber that was everywhere so plentiful. In fact many pioneers in the Maritimes

51

The stage-coach line from York (Toronto) to
Kingston, 1829.
*How long would the journey have taken at a speed
of 6 m.p.h. (allow 15 minutes for changing the horses)?*

turned from farming altogether when they realized the opportunities
offered by the trade in timber. This had very serious consequences for
both the settlements and the families involved.

It is obvious that one of the greatest problems faced by the early
settlers was that travel was exceedingly difficult, and schools, churches,
doctors, mills, and stores were quite often thirty or more miles away.
Such a distance is nothing today, but for the pioneer a place thirty
miles away might just as well have been half way around the world.

Yonge Street, which went north from Toronto as far as Lake Simcoe,
was in terrible condition as late as 1801. Unburned logs, tree stumps,
and brush lay across the roadway, and the entire road was for the most
part 'not passable for any carriage whatever on account of the logs which
lie on the street'. One unfortunate traveller who had the 'misfortune'
to use the roads of the Niagara district in the same year wrote: '[I]

esteem my escape from broken neck, legs and arms more miraculous than that of the survivors of the memorable battle of the Devil's Hole.'

The most notorious roads were the corduroy roads. When a roadway was cleared of trees, the fallen timber was laid across the road to prevent the travellers from getting stuck in the mud. The result was a terribly rough ride over uneven logs. These roads were so awful, wrote one traveller in 1837, 'that no words can give you any idea of them. We often sank in mudholes . . .; then over trunks of trees laid across swamps called corduroy roads, where my poor bones dislocated.' When this traveller reached his destination he complained that 'my hands were swelled and blistered by continually grasping with all my strength an iron bar in the front of my vehicle to prevent myself from being flung out.' It is little wonder that travel on such roads rarely exceeded three or four miles an hour.

Stage-coach service was fairly common between the various towns and villages. The one that connected Woodstock, Brantford, and Hamilton in 1810 was typical—it was driven by four horses that were changed for fresh ones every fifteen miles. The coach carried nine passengers inside while several others hung on outside, running the risk of becoming covered with mud and dust. Even for those inside the coach there was little comfort. Travellers' accounts are full of descriptions of woeful journeys that ended in dislocated limbs, bruises, and the inability to sit down for a week. In addition to the roughness of the ride, the passengers were compelled to get out and help pry the wheels out of mudholes whenever the coach got stuck.

The two best ways of travelling were on foot or by water. Travel on foot was safe and, given the amount of time spent in getting stage coaches out of the mud and changing the horses, it was probably faster. Furthermore, walking could not have been any more uncomfortable than riding in a stage coach. In 1826 Samuel Strickland received word in Peterborough that his wife, who was staying in Bowmanville, was seriously ill. He set out on foot and managed to cover a distance of fifty-eight miles in a single day, only to learn that his wife had died shortly before he arrived. Had the roads of the day been good, he would have taken the stage coach and seen his wife before she died.

Some haphazard efforts were made to improve the roadways because it was recognized that farmers needed to get their produce to town or village markets. Building and repairing roads was a very costly undertaking and so toll booths were set up along the roads to help earn money to pay for such expenditures. A house was usually attached to the toll gate for the collector and his family. A vehicle drawn by two horses was charged ten cents; each additional horse was taxed at four cents. A wagon hauled by one horse cost five cents. Each cow was taxed at two cents, while a score of sheep cost the owner a mere five cents. A man on horseback was required to pay four cents.

Just as many had suspected, the building of toll houses did not necessarily result in improved roads. The tolls became a symbol of the hardships of pioneer life. Resentment grew among the people and it was not uncommon for a farmer to ride three or four miles out of his way to avoid the 'hated tolls'. Though almost everyone agreed on the need for improvements, 'there is such a fear of . . . tolls,' wrote Mary O'Brien, an early settler in Upper Canada, 'that there are numerous petitions pouring in against improvement. This fear of tolls,' she continued, 'is no great wonder, for in the States and Lower Canada the tolls are as common as the roads are wretched.' Unfortunately neither the tolls nor the complaints of irate farmers and travellers did much to improve the roads for travel. In fact Ontario really had few roads worthy of the name until very late in the nineteenth century. Those who wished to travel by land were better off to walk or to wait until winter and use a horse-drawn sleigh.

It is little wonder that the rivers, lakes, and streams were the preferred highways in early Canada. The bateau and canoe were used extensively by the settlers as well as the Durham boat, which was introduced by American settlers in 1809. Like the bateau, the Durham boat was a flat-bottomed craft, but its rounded bow and square stern marked it as different from the bateau. The bottom was sometimes covered with iron to prevent rock damage. The Durham boat had no specific accommodation for passengers and was no more comfortable than the bateau in this respect. Like the bateau, it had sails, and the crew used long poles of white ash or hickory to get through strong currents or rapids. The Durham boat was used along the shores of the St Lawrence River and Lake Ontario to transport flour, peas, pork,

A toll gate.
*Why did settlers both complain about the condition
of the roads and about paying tolls? Were their
complaints reasonable?*

salt, potash, rum, and bales of fur. Both the Durham boats and the
bateaux made their way up and down the St Lawrence River in groups
of five or six. Thus, although serious accidents sometimes occurred, a
heavy loss of life was avoided because there was always someone to go
to the rescue.

One of the most interesting modes of water transportation was the
horse ferry. Alfred Domett, an Englishman who travelled in Canada in
1834, described it in the following way.

*The horse ferries have an odd appearance to one who has never
before seen them. The first I saw through the mist I almost mistook for
a flat black rock with a few trees or bushes upon it. It stole noiselessly
along the surface of the water, a barge like machine, with nothing to
distinguish between bow and stern, no sign of mast, sail, rope, chimney,
oars, etc. . . .*

The horse ferry had paddles that were set in motion by two to five horses who walked around and around the deck pushing a wheel as they went. The movement of the paddles propelled the boat forward. This was a safe, convenient method of travel but it was also slow. One of the last horse ferries used in Canada was the Peninsula Packet, which ran between Toronto and Ward's Island as late as 1850.

Steamships provided yet another way to travel on the St Lawrence River and Lake Ontario. There was steamship travel between Montreal and Québec as early as 1809. It took sixty-six hours to make the journey of some hundred and fifty miles. Thirty of these hours were spent at anchor because a steamer did not have lights for night travel. Ox teams were sometimes used to tow the ship through the heavy currents of certain sections of the St Lawrence. The speed was considered to be exceptionally good for those days—almost three miles an hour. The cost of the trip per person from Montreal to Québec was eight dollars. The return trip from Québec to Montreal was nine dollars; an additional charge of one dollar was levied because the current was against the ship going upriver and so it took longer to reach Montreal.

For the pioneer farmer the stage coaches, horseferries, and steamships were almost useless. He had no great need to sail from Montreal to Québec, but what he did want was a fast, safe, inexpensive way of getting his agricultural produce to the nearest market. He wanted a decent road to his nearest neighbours, to the church, to the school, and, of course, to the doctor. Steamships and stage coaches, with their schedules and fancy prices, were no answer for the backwoods farmer.

And so the canoe, the bateau, and walking remained more important as modes of transportation.

In wintertime snow-shoes or the sleigh were the easiest ways of travelling short distances. Market sleighs were used by both the farmer and the town dweller and consisted of 'two or three boards nailed together in the form of a wooden box upon runners; some straw and a buffalo skin or blanket serve for the seat; barrels of flour and baskets of eggs fill up the empty space.' Alfred Domett recounted a story in which both the usefulness of the sleigh and the primitive conditions of pioneer life are apparent. An accident occurred while a group of men were chopping wood some distance from the nearest shanty.

A 'one hoss shay'.

Richard Deedes 'cut himself badly across the instep' and was losing a lot of blood. His friends carried him to a sleigh and he was driven to the nearest house. After they waited for what seemed hours, the doctor finally arrived and 'spent some time taking up and tying the divided artery.' Domett, who was asked to provide some candlelight so that the doctor might clearly see what he was about, held the candle too close and managed to 'set the doctor's head on fire while operating'.

Like the French Canadians, the English pioneer farmers found that a winter sleighing party was a real source of pleasure. The sleigh was also a most comfortable way of travelling to visit distant friends and neighbours. Many priests and ministers used the sleigh as a convenient way of getting out to the back districts to baptize and marry the faithful. William Proudfoot was one such minister who had occasion to use the sleigh. 'One needs to be very well clothed for riding in a sleigh,' he wrote his daughter in 1832. Mr Proudfoot was deadly serious. He must have looked very odd when he ventured out in his sleigh. First he put on

a large pair of stockings down over the shoes and coming over the knee, then a pair of mocassins over all. . . . Then over a great coat must be a buffalo skin—a bearskin over the knees—a fur cap with pieces of fur over the ears—and on the hands gloves lined with fur inside and covered with fur outside—or if these are not had, then mittens or pawkies are used— Gloves of leather or wool will not do. Then a shawl tied round the neck, and a sash round the waist to keep all tight. Dressed in this manner a person may laugh at the wind. I stood the cold remarkably well. I had on two pairs of trousers, two flannel shirts, two waistcoats,—a pair of pawkies—a piece of flannel over my ears,—In this way I was perfectly comfortable in a sleigh.... In winter nobody cares for appearances, comfort is the thing.

When the minister made his trip to the settlers he held meetings and services all along the way. As soon as he arrived at a pioneer home, word was sent to friends and neighbours, who immediately left their work because this was such a rare occasion. Baptisms and marriages were often performed in groups because there were so many to be done in such a short space of time. As soon as his official duties were completed, the minister got an early start for the next settlement where the whole procedure would be repeated.

It is difficult to determine what effect the lack of regular church services had on the religious life of the pioneer communities. Whenever the minister arrived, attendance at the services was always great. This was partly because of the practical need for baptismal or marriage ceremonies. It was also because the arrival of a minister presented a good excuse for meeting socially with the neighbours. No doubt for some settlers the arrival of the minister had more social than religious significance. This probably explains why almost every minister complained bitterly about the lack of respect that was especially apparent when the pioneers insisted on bringing their dogs to the meeting and allowing them to yelp and howl throughout the sermon.

Aside from the obvious fun of sleighing and skating during the winter when farming came to a standstill, there were other highlights during the year. 'Oh the gladdest time of year' goes the rhyme,

Is the merry sugar making
When the swallows first appear
And the sleepy buds are waking!

Maple-sugar time was an event that everyone looked forward to as winter slowly thawed into spring. In fact there was a saying that 'when it freezes soundly at night, with a bright warm sun the next day, wind in the west and no sign of storm, the veins of the maples fairly thrill.'

The process of collecting syrup was begun by boring a hole in the south side of the trunk of the maple tree. Into this hole a flat piece of wood known as a spill was inserted to direct the sap into a tin pail. The best trees were the hard maples with a broad spreading top, ample roots, and a long trunk. It took almost thirty-two gallons of sap to make

58

The Peninsula Packet.
What advantage did the horse ferry have over the
other kinds of boats mentioned earlier in this book?

one gallon of sweet maple syrup. The syrup was then boiled to make the delicious maple sugar.

Generally there was a party, and, if possible, neighbours would come by to join in the merrymaking. There is an old legend that once a very long time ago, maple sugar came directly from the trees. According to this legend the Indians began to spend almost all their time leaning against the large maple trees and eating sugar. The wise man of the tribe saw that the Indians were becoming lazy and wasting all their time eating maple sugar. He begged the good Spirit to make maple sugar more difficult to procure so that his fellow tribesmen would appreciate it more and not spend all their time eating this tasty delight. The good Spirit answered his plea and so the process of making maple sugar became more complicated.

One of the nicest things about pioneer life was the co-operation that existed among the settlers. When Thomas Need decided to build a saw mill near Bobcaygeon in 1834, his neighbours and friends came from all over the district to give him a hand. 'They assembled in great force and all worked together in great harmony and good will, notwith-standing their different stations in life.' Everyone continued working and 'when the last rafter was fixed, a bottle of whisky was broken . . . then the party separated well satisfied with their day's work.'

A barn-raising bee.
How many families do you think might have been helping?

These 'bees', as they were called, were held to cut lumber, to clear land, and to build barns and homes. The ladies had quilting bees when all the women of the settlement would assemble at one house with their materials. In an area where a six-month-old newspaper was considered a rare treat, the bee was not only a welcome source of companionship and assistance, it was an excellent way of passing on important news and information to other members of the community. If possible the end of a bee was marked with a plentiful meal. At Thomas Need's bee to raise his saw mill, pies and cakes were served as well as 'a roast pig and a boiled leg of mutton, a dish of fish, a large cold mutton pie, cold ham and cold roast mutton, mashed potatoes and beans and carrots, a large rice pudding, a large bread and butter pudding, and currant and gooseberry tarts.'

After everyone had eaten, a dance was usually held in the barn. The dance would last well into the night. When it finally came to an end, each family gathered their tools and whatever else they had brought and headed home, tired but pleased with the day's effort.

4 Roads and Villages

Just as the first settlements in New France grew up close to the best means of transportation, the St Lawrence, so in what is now Ontario transportation was an important factor in determining the location of the first villages and towns. In the days before roads and rails, the waterways—the lakes and rivers—were still the major highways; as roads were built, villages or towns grew at points along these lines of communication also.

There were a number of reasons for the founding of a village or town: the earliest in Ontario were founded as military and administrative centres for the province. Others developed because they were natural centres of trade for the surrounding district. Sometimes an enterprising man built a mill in a favourable location around which a settlement eventually developed. When roads were built, the wayside inn or tavern, like the mill, often formed an attraction around which a village might grow.

The settlement of Carleton Place, near Ottawa, is typical of village development. In 1818 Edmund Morphy built a home near the rapids of a river. A couple of years later his two sons built houses nearby. In the meantime Morphy sold the waterpower on his property to a man named Bolton who wished to construct a mill. Once the mill was in

A mill, Manotick, Ontario.
As well as being a means of transportation, the waterways provided another important service to settlers. What was it? For what other purposes are Canada's water resources used today?

operation settlers of the area arrived daily on the scene to grind their wheat. The presence of so many potential customers encouraged William Moore to set up a blacksmith's shop. Next came a tannery, a potash 'works', a general store, and a hotel or 'groggery'. Such was the founding of Carleton Place—today an important village on the Canadian Pacific Railway line.

The village of Minden, on the other hand, owes its birth to the building of the Bobcaygeon Road. At the junction of the road and the Gull River a few log houses were built by newly arrived settlers. In due time, recalled the Reverend George Kenney, 'there was a small store in a little log house and another in a board shanty roofed with boards. This place also served as a stopping place for such travellers as had the hardihood to put up at the tavern . . . and there the people assembled for worship. This was the germ of the future county town.' It was not long before Minden became 'the centre for the fine district surrounding it, and Mr Daniel Buck, who keeps the tavern there, has his hands full . . . to entertain his guests.'

A typical village might have a foundry, a tannery, a general store, and taverns for travellers. Every village had its artisans to supply the needs of the community, such as shoemakers, blacksmiths, carpenters, and cabinet makers. It might also boast the presence of a doctor, a dentist, and a lawyer. Eventually the town would build its own school, have one or more churches, and a post office somewhere on the main street. These settlements served the needs of the struggling settlers of the surrounding countryside.

The early industry of these little towns was especially important because it provided employment for the men of the area as well as supplying the basic needs of the backwoods farmer when he made a visit to the village either to purchase goods or have a harness repaired. The foundry, for example, was really a small machine shop where skilled workers made land rollers, wagons, sleighs, hand straw cutters, and scufflers. Many of these items were essential to the farmers of the district. The village blacksmith, contrary to popular myth, did much more than just shoe horses. He made carriages of all types, both for use in the town and in the countryside. The most common vehicle was the 'buggy', a light carriage with large wheels and room for two occupants. It was particularly suited to the bumpy and muddy roads that character-ized this era of development. When the blacksmith was not busy building carriages, he repaired all sorts of equipment, from buggy and wagon wheels to a bobsled that needed a new runner. In addition, the blacksmith also made such small items as hoes, rakes, shovels, and axes.

The tanning of hides for leather was a necessary and important industry in the early days of settlement. During the process of curing, however, the tannery was a good place to stay away from. The smell of the hides boiling in tanning liquid certainly had nothing to recommend it to passersby. Frequently farmers who lacked the necessary cash to have their hides tanned entered into special agreements with the tanner. Sometimes the farmer would bring two hides, one for the tanner and one for himself.

Perhaps one of the most interesting industries to us today was feather cleaning. Feathers were used to stuff the pillows and mattresses of these early settlers. In Hanover, Ontario, the local feather-cleaner had a huge wire cage that he filled with feathers. Steam was turned on and the

A village store built around 1820.
What kinds of things are sold in village stores today
that were not sold in 1820?

cage whirled rapidly for several minutes. The soiled water ran out of the cage through a pipe inserted at one end. When the feathers were clean, the steam was turned off and the cage continued to whirl until the feathers were completely dry. The dry, clean feathers were then packed into bags to sell for mattress stuffing.

Although it does not properly fall under the category of local industry, the general store was important enough to the life of the village to deserve special mention. In the first place the general store sold almost everything a village resident or a visiting farmer might need. On the crowded and often unorganized shelves of a typical general store the prospective buyer could find a door hinge or an axe, a barrel of flour or a pair of shoes. Speaking of shoes, there is some evidence to suggest that it was not considered proper for a respectable lady to try on boots or shoes at the store. Numerous entries on general store ledgers indicate that female customers always took home two pairs of footwear and then returned the pair least suitable.

The prices of goods at the general store seem very inexpensive by

Sawmill, Hackston, 1840.
*For what uses had timber become a valuable
resource at this time?*

today's standards. It is important to bear in mind that few people of the day had much cash and most sales were on credit until harvest time. Sugar, for example, was ten cents a pound; eggs were eight cents a dozen, geese five cents a pound, and cheese was a bargain at twelve cents a pound. Slippers were fifteen cents a pair, a bonnet sold for twenty-five cents, and a man could purchase a good tweed suit for less than five dollars. It was not uncommon for a store to display prominently signs like the following in the section of a store where men's clothing was sold.

Pants, yes, we were near forgetting that pants were made for men and not for women; woman was made for man and not for pants.
Such advertising would undoubtedly anger the 'liberated' woman of today.

As well as selling goods, the local merchants performed other important services in these early towns. 'The storekeepers,' wrote Mrs Traill in 1832, 'are the merchants and bankers of the places in which they reside. Almost all money matters are transacted by them, and they are often men of landed property and consequence.' Most people depended upon credit to purchase their supplies. The storekeeper usually extended credit to his customers until harvest time. The farmer might then pay his debt to the storekeeper in bushels of wheat or oats, and the storekeeper would then arrange to sell these grains to the local miller. If the farmer was certain of a better price for his produce in a larger town, he would take as much of his wheat as possible by wagon to the town, collect his cash, and then pay off his debt to the village storekeeper. In times of crop failure, the kindly storekeeper was very often the only person who stood between the farmer and starvation.

The doctor, like the storekeeper, was a very important resident in every town and village. He tended not only those who lived in the village itself, but also as many of those who lived in the district as possible. When a child took sick in the middle of the night and the worried parents sent for the doctor, they were confident that he would come regardless of the time, regardless of the weather. The doctor rode on horseback when he could to visit his patients, and walked when it was impossible to take a horse. There is a story told of one Dr James Lightbody who had the oddest method of preparing medicine. Often, in the presence of his patients, he stirred the remedy with his none-too-clean fingers—and then put his finger to his mouth to sample it, remarking that a doctor should always taste his own medicine. Despite his unsanitary method of preparing medication, the good doctor was quite successful at curing the sick of the area.

As the towns and villages grew they attracted more and more permanent residents. The arrival of a dentist was a sure sign of a town's importance. Before the establishment of professional standards in 1868, anyone who wished to become a dentist simply hung up his shingle and went to work. To be fair, though, many dentists worked as apprentices with other practising members of their profession before going into business for themselves. Usually the dentist arrived at his office, which was part of his house as well, at seven o'clock in the morning. Extractions were a painful matter in the days before gas or freezing, although the victim might be given a stiff drink of strong whisky to ease his suffering. By the 1860s dentists were able to solicit business by promising 'painless extractions with laughing gas'.

66

A well-to-do house in Bridgeport, Ontario.
What were the advantages and disadvantages of the
horse and buggy as a means of travel?

Like the practice of dentistry, the drugstore as a separate business came later to most towns and villages. This was largely owing to the fact that all doctors kept their own supply of drugs and prepared their own medicines for their patients. The first drugstore came to the village of Hanover in 1864. It contained patent medicines, salts, different brands of pain killers, blood bitters, sassafras, hair oil, condition powders, and, as the sign advertised, 'physics of all kinds for man and beast'. Many of these strange potions were reputed to have marvellous healing powers, and local residents swore to their effectiveness. The store also probably carried such wonder drugs as 'Carrolia', which was guaranteed to make whiskers and mustaches grow on the smoothest face or chin.

For those who lived and worked in the village, life was certainly an improvement over the lot of the backwoods farmer. True, stumps in the streets were not an uncommon sight, and the roads were a mud trap in the spring and fall. Even the houses were roughly constructed in a manner similar to those of the pioneer farmers who lived in the surrounding district. Cows casually wandered in the streets, and every house, in addition to a large vegetable garden and a few chickens, had 'sows and pigs and with them the necessary appendages, a pool to wallow in etc.' Dogs posed a real problem in the village streets and the editor of the Chatham newspaper in 1842 echoed the sentiments of many residents when he demanded that something should be done. 'Turn your eye which way you will, a drove of these animals will be observed,' he wrote, 'either chasing some unfortunate stranger of their species round a corner, or engaged in some other recreation more disgusting and annoying to the modest and well-disposed portion of her Majesty's liege subjects of this town.'

Despite these shortcomings, however, those who lived in the towns or villages had the advantage of social contact with their neighbours who lived only a few blocks rather than miles away. For the women life in the village clearly had much to offer. There was still the drudgery of washing the family's clothing by hand and trying to keep the house clean without the assistance of a vacuum cleaner, but these women could take a break from their daily routine and walk through the muddy streets to the general store. Along the way there was always an opportunity to stop and chat with other village residents. Once at the general store, the shopper could simply browse or buy some flour, clothes, or even a luxury like 'imported' perfume.

Most women found their days filled with sewing, cooking, and tending to the family's needs. Some also managed to help their husbands in the store or to keep business records for them. Only a very few were free to spend their afternoons sipping tea and exchanging recipes with a friend. For all the women, though, there was great comfort in knowing that during a family crisis or a more general emergency they would not be alone or helpless. A midwife or a doctor attended the birth of their children and watched over them in times of sickness. And almost as important was the knowledge that a minister or a trusted friend was always nearby and ready to offer solace during trying times.

Chatham, 1838.
Compare the construction of the houses with that of
the shanties built by the backwoods farmers. In what
ways had people become better off since the arrival
of the United Empire Loyalists fifty years before?

Most of the men who lived in the village either owned their own shop or business or worked for someone who did. Like the farmer, they worked long hours. When the day's work was finished, though, the blacksmith or the shopkeeper might stop off at the local tavern for a couple of pints and a short chat before going home for supper. He did not have to worry about his family when he was away from home. He knew that his children were receiving a standard education and that the facilities of a doctor, dentist, and minister were within a reasonable distance from his home. He did not have to worry about his wife's being lonely and, perhaps, cracking under the strain. No, life in the town or village freed men from the many worries faced by the backwoods farmer.

The social activities offered by these small centres were also an important attraction. The town tavern was not only a pub to the people

Village social life.
What evidence is there that farming is being carried on nearby?

of the town and a place to meet friends. It was there that the first church services were usually held. Political meetings and banquets were also housed by the local tavern.

The building of a permanent church marked an important point in the growth of a village. The first church, like other buildings of that time, was usually quite small and constructed of logs. Donated materials and the volunteer labour of the residents made the building of the church a community effort. There was more than a little pride in the village when the church was finally completed. The people of the village of Haliburton seemed not to notice that when Dr Peake led the choir and played the accordion at the weekly church service the repertoire was limited to two songs. In fact, the walls of the little church echoed with the rising voices of the congregation.

Like the first church, the village school was a co-operative effort. It was constructed of logs; the floor was of boards, whenever they could be

A one-room schoolhouse.
*What are the advantages and disadvantages of
having children of all ages taught together?*

found; and the roof was made of oak clapboards or soft elm bark. A
bark roof was durable and effective against the rain, but in winter it
afforded little protection from the snow. There was usually a wood
stove that tried in vain to keep the classroom warm. One teacher was
specially noted for the fact that 'on cold mornings he had the children
march around the room singing the multiplication tables to the tune
of Yankee Doodle until they got warm.' The schools were always short
of textbooks and sometimes it was even difficult to find enough pencils
for the students to begin their exercises. The quality of education in
these early one-room school houses cannot be compared to today. In
some cases the teacher knew very little more than some of the advanced
students. By the standards of the day, though, the very presence of a
school house and a teacher was a mark of progress.

School attendance was not compulsory in those days and if something
exciting like a fire or a circus happened in the area, not even the teacher

was likely to show up that day. Fires were an unhappy occurrence since all the houses and shops were wooden and the firefighting equipment was still very primitive. But for the young people of the town a fire was a stirring spectacle to view.

All the firefighters were volunteers who were summoned to the scene of destruction by a church bell or the loud shouts of neighbours. In some villages, local law required every resident to hang two pails or buckets outside for use in case of a fire. Fire wardens were appointed to organize the fight and everyone was bound by law to obey their orders. In Cobourg there were two volunteer fire brigades in the 1860s and 1870s. The competition between the two brigades reached the point where fires were being deliberately set in unused or rundown buildings to provide excitement. This may seem strange today, but less than ten years ago the small village of Brechin, Ontario, purchased a brand new fire engine. With much the same motivation as those people

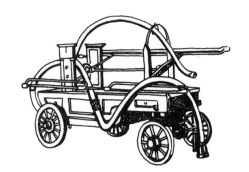

Fire engine presented to Toronto in 1837. Below: The first fire engine in Toronto, the 'York', 1826. It was manned by eight men on each side.

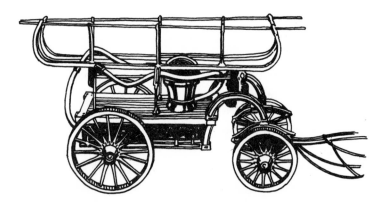

had who started the fires in Cobourg over a hundred years before, the Brechin Fire Department deliberately set a vacant old house on fire and invited the people of Brechin and the nearby villages to bring their lawn chairs and watch the Fire Department in action.

Most towns and villages had an annual parade-day for their volunteer firemen and the entire brigade would march in full uniform, if they had one. All the fire equipment was polished for the occasion and then inspected by the village council and other interested residents. After the parade a supper and dance were held, making this one of the great social events of the year.

The arrival of a circus was another social highlight of the year. Most of the shows, like the one that came to Chatham in 1846, boasted a number of acrobats and clowns, including a famous contortionist 'known as the youth without bones'. In addition to these wonders there was the well-known strong man, Yankee Samson, who could carry hundred-pound weights by his hair and bend a four-inch iron rod across his arm. In the town of Hanover one young boy managed to get close enough to touch a real live elephant and immediately became the envy of his friends.

The circus usually made the town a virtual hive of activity for the day or so that it stayed. The population swelled to the bursting point as everyone who lived within a reasonable distance flocked to see the wonders of Yankee Samson or the deadly cobra. When the townsfolk arose from their slumber the next day, the circus and all the magic it had brought with it had vanished sometime during the night.

For older village residents the Agricultural Fair or Harvest Festival was much more important than the arrival of a circus. Farmers from all over the county brought their best produce or finest animals to exhibit. Each man secretly hoped to drive off with at least one or more prize ribbons at the conclusion of the exhibition. For their part, the ladies of the area exhibited handmade quilts and fancy dresses, and some say the finest baked goods anywhere. When Haliburton began what was to become an annual Agricultural Fair in 1865, everyone in the village and half the residents of the surrounding district participated in the exhibition. 'The exhibits,' reported the newspaper, 'were arranged before James Erskine's blacksmith shop with the ladies' work shown to

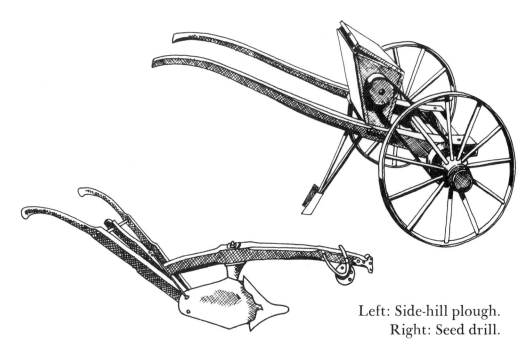

Left: Side-hill plough.
Right: Seed drill.

advantage on a line stretched above a carpenter's workbench, the top of which held two pairs of ox-bows and a complete ox yoke with wooden bow-keys all constructed by local artisans. Under the workbench,' the reporter noticed, 'turnips, potatoes and other garden produce including two fine pumpkins and some corn grown by Mr David Sawyer.' The agricultural fair, like the fire and the circus, was an important part of community life. Such activities promoted co-operation and close personal contact with the other residents of the village. This interaction, more than any other single factor, made life in these small centres preferable to the loneliness and isolation faced by the backwoods farmer.

There were many occasions during the year when celebrations and fun were the order of the day. Militia parades, for example, were an important part of life since all men from sixteen to sixty-five years of age were members of the militia. Parade-day consisted of a little military drill and a lot of horse racing, gambling, and hard drinking. Some men came with only part of their uniform and the oddest assortment of firearms. The general appearance of the militia inspired little confidence in the ability of the group to 'save' the country in case of attack from the United States. Some critics described the group as 'particoloured and curiously equipped'. Others, although more harsh, were probably closer to the mark when they described parade-day as a 'laughter-stirring spectacle'. Despite these criticisms, the members of the militia and those who came to join in the day's festivities thoroughly enjoyed themselves.

Village life had much to offer its residents during the nineteenth century. A sense of community, companionship, and some of the goods and services that the people had been familiar with before arriving in Canada were all part of the village milieu. In addition, the village performed a vital function in the development of Canada by servicing the needs of the surrounding agricultural district.

It would be a mistake, however, to equate village life a hundred years ago with that of today. For one thing, the streets were little better than the stump-ridden and bumpy trails that characterized the countryside. Few villages had plank sidewalks, and when the spring rains came the streets turned into muddy rivulets. In the summer, swirling dust filled the air until it was almost impossible to breathe. A short walk to the general store and back often required a complete change of clothing. Life might have continued in this way indefinitely had it not been for the invention of the steam engine. A revolution in transportation was accompanied by an equally startling change in the lifestyle and pattern of settlement of Canadians.

5 Rails and Steam

Railway building in Canada excited the imagination and stirred the hopes of townsfolk and farmers alike. Although railways were discussed and even planned as early as the 1830s, it was not until the 1850s that the real boom in railway building began. With this boom came important changes in the everyday life of the people and the future development of the country itself. For some, life would improve beyond their wildest expectations, but for others the failure to attract a railway to town meant the eventual decline and, in some cases, the disappearance of the place they had once called home.

To the farmers the railway had a special meaning. After the fall harvest, the farmers of western Ontario, for example, toiled over 'the most horrible roads, through dismal dreary swamps on their way to Galt, and even as far as Hamilton, with a few bags of wheat, for the purpose of obtaining as much money as would pay their taxes, and procure some of the ordinary necessities of life for their families. . . .' When the cost of the trip was deducted from their earnings there was often little cash left. All this would change—or so most farmers thought —when the iron horse came to the countryside.

To those who lived in small villages the railway would bring information about the larger world and renewed contact with friends and old neighbours, sons and married daughters, who lived in other towns and villages. The old man who complained bitterly because 'there are no good roads [and] we have often to wade through mud and swamps for many miles together and except in sleighing season find it almost impossible to go any distance' saw the railway as a means of solving the more general problems of transportation. But the hope of prosperity was the real key to the great support for expensive railway building schemes in all the small centres. Increased land values, an influx of population, and higher prices for agricultural produce were in many minds synonymous with railways.

Canadian businessmen, too, were favourably disposed to the building of railways. They were primarily interested in tapping the trade of the American mid-west. A fast, efficient, and inexpensive form of transportation could make this goal a reality. These businessmen were certain that they could lure American trade to Canada for one very good reason: England did not tax goods coming from Canada and the other colonies as heavily as 'foreign' goods. If the American farmer and others were to ship their produce via Canadian railways to the east coast where ships would be waiting to transport the goods to England, the Americans too could enjoy the advantages of the Canadian tax 'preference'. The plan was a good one. Unfortunately, in 1846, long before the Canadian rail system had been completed, the English withdrew all taxes on imported goods. No longer was it beneficial for American farmers to ship their produce through Canada. But this setback for Canadian businessmen did not dampen their enthusiasm for railway construction; they still believed that railways would usher in an era of unbounded economic prosperity.

Money to fund the construction of railways came from the government in the form of monetary and land grants. Town and village councils were also generous in their cash subsidies and land grants. A small proportion of the total cost of construction was collected through the sale of stocks to the public. A. T. Galt, an early railway promoter in Canada, boasted of the 'good faith and hearty co-operation of every resident' in the particular area through which his company intended to build a line. Despite their enthusiasm these people lacked sufficient cash to become shareholders. To raise money for the railway and to

The 'Lady Elgin', the first locomotive used in
Ontario, 1852.

give the people of the district a sense of participation in the project,
arrangements were made to have the farmers of the area purchase shares
by supplying the construction gangs with meat, flour, butter, or eggs
at a fixed schedule of prices.

In addition to financial problems, the early railway builders were
confronted with their own inexperience in construction. Most companies relied on the English railway system as a model for construction
in Canada. Unfortunately they sometimes failed to recognize that the
differences in geography and climate had serious consequences for the
construction of railways. For example, the temperature range in Canada
between mid-summer and mid-winter was far greater than in England
and very often caused the wooden rails to warp and buckle. The curious
shape of the curled-up rails led to their nickname 'snake-rails'.

Snow removal from the tracks was yet another problem that Canadian
railroaders had to contend with. Sometimes horses were used to pull
'snowed-in engines' along the track. Wooden ploughs attached to the
front of the engine were sometimes useful in light snow. In blizzards,
when the drifted snow reached depths of two or three feet, the train
simply came to a halt. For those passengers who wished exercise, shovels
were provided and an attempt to dig out the train began in earnest.
Such efforts were usually a failure and the passengers simply reconciled

A snow plough.
How are the tracks kept free of snow today?

themselves to the fact. They would remain stranded until help arrived in the form of another engine, or a rise in temperature.

The actual construction of the various railroads usually began with the employment of local residents. As work progressed, more men, especially skilled workmen, were required. The labour for the construction of the Irondale, Bancroft, and Ottawa Railway was initially supplied by area residents 'aided by some Italians, but the higher wages offered by the logging firms soon forced the company to depend on 300 immigrants, mostly Italian.'

Skilled labour with experience in railroad construction came primarily from England because it was the first country to build railroads. Stone masons, carpenters, engine drivers, and fitters were brought to Canada to work on construction at a salary of eight to ten shillings a day. Passage fare to Canada was loaned to prospective workers, who were promised a yearly bonus of one to two pounds and guaranteed at least five years of employment. One old-timer recalled 'watching men surveying for the Grand Trunk Railway. My eldest brother, Clinton,'

79

A surveying crew.
Why was the work of the surveyors necessary?

Making a road bed.
Why are road beds sometimes raised above the
surrounding terrain?

he said, 'was engaged in clearing the way for the roadbed. This land was purchased from the farmers, and they were given the timber rights if they would clear it away. Local men were hired to help the gang of labourers—mostly Irish—in the construction of the road. They employed horses and scrapers for most of the work, a very crude method. . . .'

Conditions on the work gangs were often scandalous. Deaths from accidents and disease were so commonplace that few remarked on these happenings. During the 1850s, for example, a railway was constructed from Cobourg to Peterborough. The tracks followed the meanderings of the Cobourg Creek and then crossed Rice Lake. The damp terrain and poor housing facilities for the construction gang gave rise to an epidemic of cholera and fever that resulted in the loss of many lives.

The scarcity of financing for many of these early railroads led almost inevitably to poor construction and the choice of basically unsound routes. It was cheaper to build a long, winding railroad than to build along a direct route that might involve heavy capital costs for blasting through rock or for bridging a deep ravine. The line that was constructed from Summerside to Charlottetown in Prince Edward Island is typical of many small railroads built in Canada from the 1830s to the turn of the century. One critic complained that 'the contractors, for the double purpose of saving the expense of blasting or digging, and increasing the mileage and with it the contract price, invariably carried the road around any rising rather than over or through it.' When the project was finally completed, the trip overland proved to be 'one of the most disturbing experiences anyone can have'.

The little narrow gauge line twists and doubles until the traveller reaches the verge of sea sickness. It is popularly supposed that at a certain exceptionally fantastic curve, the conductor, standing upon the rear platform, can and does offer a chew of tobacco to the engineer on the locomotive [at the front].

One of the first railways constructed in Canada was the Erie and Ontario line. It was designed as a portage route around Niagara Falls from Queenston to Chippewa. The road was completed in 1839, but the grades were too steep for the little engines to pull the cars. To overcome this obstacle a rather novel solution was adopted. The

81

A CPR construction train, 1891.
*Suggest how the men would be accommodated
inside the train.*

following traveller's account written in 1845 explains the way in which the Erie and Ontario operated. 'You are whirled along, not by steam, but by three trotting horses at a rapid rate along a wood road till you reach the falls.' It is ironic that this railroad was able to operate only because of the horse—the animal it would gradually replace in importance.

Every town and village through which the railway passed dreamed of becoming a large and prosperous city of importance. The arrival of the first train was a very special event marked by colourful parades and excited speeches. When the first train pulled into Brantford on Friday, January 13, 1854, Thomas Cowhers, a local tinsmith, was inspired to write a poem to commemorate the occasion.

> *The iron horse has reached Cayuga's height as near:*
> *Look out, ye men of Brantford now, for soon he will here.*
> *He brings with him a mighty load, by way before him feels,*
> *As slowly o'er the new hard track he moves his pondering wheels.*

Some of the excitement of the day was captured by a reporter on the local newspaper, the *Expositor*.

Laying track.
What purpose do the wooden sleepers serve? Are tracks built the same way today?

Shortly after 2 p.m. the trains arrived and were received with loud cheers, firing of cannon and every demonstration of joy. There were three locomotives, the first with one passenger car, the second with five, and the third with one, all well filled. About five hundred, we understand, came over from Buffalo, including a large number of Buffalo firemen who made a very good appearance in their splendid uniforms.

Almost twelve thousand people assembled in Brantford that historic day. When the speeches and luncheons at last came to an end, the crowds were treated to a lively dance. As the day finally drew to a close a wonderful display of fireworks brightened the sky as a symbol of the bright future for the little town.

When the Grand Trunk Railway arrived in Belleville in 1856, there were similar crowds and festivities. The *Weekly Intelligencer*, however, was more concerned with the hard economic facts of the new railroad than with reporting the celebrations. 'Belleville has at last been placed upon the great highway,' predicted the editor, 'by the opening of the Grand Trunk Railway. The event is one of utmost importance to us

83

On the way from Prescott to Ottawa.
*The horses are waiting to pick up passengers going
to Ottawa. What method would you use to get from
Prescott to Ottawa today?*

as a town.' In the first place, 'merchants and tradesmen no longer will have to lay in a heavy six months' stock of goods to keep supplies until the season arrives for the opening of navigation. . . .' Although the editor did not know it at the time, Belleville was to become a divisional point for the GTR. Locomotive shops would one day be built and in time the railway would become the town's largest employer.

The dynamic growth of the sleepy little village of St Mary's, Ontario, was also a product of the Grand Trunk Railway. When the track eventually reached St Mary's, the little town became the bustling shipping centre for the great area of newly opened farmland in Perth and south Huron counties. William Johnston, who arrived in the area to take up a farm, described the town after the arrival of the railroad.

On the streets could be seen every day a dozen of grain buyers, all busy, with long strings of loaded wagons pouring into the town from all directions. During autumn the market square was for several hours each day blocked with teams, and extending down Queen Street as far as Wellington was a mass of men and horses, with wheat and other products awaiting an opportunity to move onward.

A similar story of growth is told for the village of Tavistock. Before the arrival of the railway it consisted of a few scattered houses. As soon as the railway passed through the settlement, the number of houses began to multiply rapidly. A church soon made its appearance on the scene, along with a post office. In less than ten years the scattered little houses had become a thriving village of eight hundred residents.

Although most of the towns and villages echoed sentiments similar to that of the *Peterborough Review* when it heralded the arrival of the first trains as 'one of the proudest days that the sister towns of Cobourg and Peterborough have ever seen . . .', some would later regret this premature optimism. The railway boom would not last forever and some of the feverish economic activity that first accompanied the arrival of the iron horse was doomed to dry up. The editor of the Goderich newspaper expressed some reservation about the town's future long before others were to become critical of this new transportation network and the changes it would bring about. 'The very people themselves have become changed,' stated the editor. 'Instead of the slow and easy John Bull mode of procedure, the merchant, mechanic, and the farmers drew up their energy to railroad speed.'

Peterborough was one town that expressed nothing but confidence in the railroad. Time was to confirm all its great expectations. Wheat, wool, and potash were shipped south to Toronto with the greatest ease. These exports reached a value of half a million dollars annually. Sawn lumber was also a moneymaker for the farmers who lived in the district around the town. Every farm still had acres of trees that could now be turned into cash income for the farmer. In fact so much lumber was hauled in wagons to the Peterborough station that sawdust became a major source of pollution in the town.

The advantages of railroad development were certainly not lost on Toronto. In 1853 Toronto businessmen were praising railroads for ushering in a new age of economic activity. Each new line constructed seemed to bring greater benefits to the city. The Northern railroad to Lake Huron, for example, consisted of a 'steam engine with a commodious passenger car and several freight cars'. Each day the train

A passenger train, 1884.
What is the man in the foreground holding?

made a trip 'to the neighbourhood of Newmarket, and already the advantages of the road are being felt in the City; by this conveyance large quantities of firewood are being brought down and sold at reduced prices.' The railway clearly broadened the patterns of distribution in every area through which it travelled. The importance of freight far overshadowed passenger travel in the early days of railroading.

Passenger travel, for the most part, was not a particularly pleasant experience, although no one could deny that it was exciting. Few trains travelled on a precise schedule, and a prospective passenger had only to stand by the side of the track and wave a handkerchief to bring the train to a halt and safely step aboard. One early traveller recorded in her diary that 'none of the trains on this side of the Atlantic connect, so we had to wait every now and then an hour or more, and they are always after their time. I know of nothing more irritating,' she continued, 'than travelling in this country.'

In addition to unscheduled stops and late arrivals, the average speed of the summer trains rarely exceeded twenty miles an hour on the flat stretches. All the locomotives burned wood, which added little to the comfort of the passengers. The initial train from Lindsay, for example, 'consisted of a bell-shaped engine which devoured four foot logs at an astonishing rate.' It was quite common for the engineer to stop the train and enlist the aid of passengers to replenish the supply of fuel in the nearby forest.

Although all the engines had a bell-shaped funnel with a screen, sparks and cinders were unpleasant for the passengers. To make the journey less hazardous many passengers carried Braid's Spark Arrester, which was guaranteed to protect the traveller from burns. The danger of flying sparks, however, proved to be a real menace to the forests adjacent to the rail lines. Mary Anne, the first engine on the Irondale, Bancroft & Ottawa Railway, belched forth a cloud of sparks that kindled blazes along the route of her maiden trip.

The first passenger cars were flat roofless structures with wooden benches for the occupants. Without protection from wind, rain, or even the hot summer sun, early train travel left much to be desired. Even later, when passenger cars were completely covered, much as they are today, seating arrangements were not designed for relaxation. 'In going from Montreal to Toronto the traveller had to sit bolt upright for sixteen or eighteen hours until every bone in his body ached and each particular bone seemed to have had a quarrel with his fellow-bones— all feeling as if they had engaged in a pitched battle.'

By the late 1860s one English visitor was able to report that passenger cars 'are like large caravans, some forty feet long and not like the English ones. . . . I have counted forty-four people in one carriage. . . . Wood is used instead of coal and the nuisance from "smuts" is intolerable. You will get nothing to eat or drink on the way but the vilest of compounds and no time to stow them. A cup of tea, if you don't sit down to drink it, is 25 cents. . . .' Twenty years later passengers were much more positive in their descriptions of railway comforts. 'Our travelling,' said one gentleman, 'is at an average rate of thirty miles an hour. In the train dining car you can get a pretty good dinner for 75 cents—soup, salmon, lamb, four kinds of vegetables (including green peas), apple-tart, and dessert.' Passenger travel in these early years was obviously a story of improvements.

One thing that did not show marked improvement was the fate of those who rode the trains during the winter. For one thing, most of the cars were extremely cold and temperatures inside were often recorded at below freezing. For the most part passengers brought heavy blankets to wrap themselves in while they squeezed as close to the stove as possible. If the snow on the track was too deep to permit the train to travel safely, the engineer simply halted the engine to wait for help from the nearest divisional point. Sometimes the passengers were able to seek refuge at a nearby farmhouse for a few hours. Sometimes they simply shivered in the cold passenger cars. Although Thomas' Snow Exterminator was advertised as a sure way of removing snow from the tracks, the number of snowbound trains in these early years testifies to its hopeless inadequacy.

Accidents on these early railroads were frequent, though not nearly as frequent as one might expect, given the quality of the workmanship and the extremes of climate faced by the engineer. One common problem faced by all the lines was the presence of stray cattle on the tracks. In one instance, near the town of Lobo, the engineer saw a number of cattle on the track about half a mile ahead. Rather than stop the train and push the cattle off to the side, the engineer speeded up in an attempt to frighten the creatures off the track. Unfortunately one stubborn cow refused to move. As a consequence a number of cars were derailed and thrown down a steep embankment. Several German immigrants who were on their way to new settlements in the area were killed and many others were injured. There is evidence to suggest that in some cases, farmers deliberately drove their cattle onto the tracks and hoped that they would be killed by a passing train. It was more profitable, it seems, to collect damages for dead cattle from the railway company than to ship the animals to market.

Farmers proved to be a problem to railroad companies in another

The 'Albion'
built 1854.

way as well. Often farmers helped themselves to whatever they needed
from the tracks to improve or repair their fences. The various railroad
companies tried to cope with such actions by sending out repair crews
as frequently as possible. The railroads needed the farmers, especially
those who owned forests or woodlots adjacent to the tracks. Since the
average train burned about fifteen cents of wood per mile, railroads
depended on the goodwill of the farmers to provide access to supplies
of wood.

Early railroading in Canada is really a story of trial and error. Many
costly mistakes were made; a lot of money was lost and many expectations remained unfulfilled. And yet it is also apparent that the age of
railroads did bring prosperity and growth to many towns and villages.
Generally speaking, those villages and small towns that were not
important enough to attract a railway and that remained dependent
on roads were doomed. It was not until the automobile became widely
used that places away from the rail lines would have another chance
to develop.

The rise of the railroad and the decline of the stage-coach in
importance had serious consequences for the wayside inns and hotels
that dotted the countryside. Between 1871 and 1881 almost forty such
establishments disappeared in one county alone. And with the demise

of some of these businesses went the small hamlets that had grown up around them.

For the farmer, on the other hand, the railroad meant increased prosperity. In the first place, proximity to the line greatly enlarged the potential market for the farmer's produce. Now it was possible to ship wheat or cattle to urban centres that were miles away from the farm. Secondly, it meant that the farmer could choose to send his goods to the area where prices were highest instead of being at the mercy of local buyers. The weeks that the farmer of the past had wasted in transporting his produce over the horrendous roads of the province could now be put to more profitable use. Like the town or village resident, the farmer whose property was close to the rail line also benefited from an increase in the value of his land. At the same time the farmer was now able to buy manufactured goods that were shipped from far-away cities.

In addition, these early ventures in railroading established a pattern in politics that was to continue for some time. In Stratford, for example, the relationship becomes clear. The Grand Trunk Railway built large workshops that provided employment for a large number of workers and resulted in a rapid increase in population in the town. Since the majority of Stratford residents depended upon the railroad for income, they gave their support to the Conservative Party, which strongly advocated railway development. Foremen in the Grand Trunk machine shops actively canvassed on the job for the Conservatives, and all who wished to stay employed enthusiastically pledged their support. This relationship between the Conservative Party and railway building was to continue through the history of railroad development in Canada.

Despite the human and financial costs that accompanied railroad building, there are many who would argue that these early experiments were a necessary prelude to the large-scale schemes to link Canada from coast to coast in the post-Confederation era.

6 Trains and Towns

'He's gone clean crazy. He is talking of running a railway from the Atlantic to the Pacific and next he will be talking about a railway to the moon.' This was the opinion of old Judge Mallock when he first heard someone talk of a transcontinental railway that would span the breadth of Canada from coast to coast. The old judge was not alone in his thinking.

Few Canadians were able to visualize the vastness of the distance between the Atlantic and the Pacific. Few dreamed of the terrible hardships that men would be asked to endure in spanning this expanse with steel tracks. Still fewer imagined that the project would be successfully completed by 1885. Despite the odds, the Canadian Pacific Railroad (CPR) was built and remains in some sense a symbol of the spirit and daring of those who believed in and worked towards its success.

And surely this gamble on the future of Canada was warranted. The completion of the line would bring prosperity and new settlers to the empty acres of the West, or so it was thought at the time. The trials of the pioneers who had struggled along muddy trails by wagon or on foot to purchase a backwoods farm in Ontario would not be repeated in the newly opened farming areas of Manitoba, Saskatchewan, and

91

A supply train for a construction camp in the Rockies.
*What especial difficulties would be encountered in
building a railroad through mountains?*

Alberta. These new lands would be populated by settlers who arrived
not by twos or threes but by the thousands on a new national railway.

Once it had been decided that a national railway should indeed be
built, the first problem, and the one that would recur with the most
alarming frequency, was money. Throughout the construction of the
CPR financial ruin was a real and constant threat. Estimates for construction were not elastic enough to absorb the demands for higher wages
and the spiralling costs of materials. Time and time again the company
had to appeal to the government for assistance. That this assistance
was given is an indication of the government's faith in the 'national
benefits' that would inevitably accompany the completion of the
railway.

John A. Macdonald, the Prime Minister of Canada during this time,
and some of his contemporaries saw the railroad as an essential
ingredient in binding together Canada from the Atlantic Provinces
to British Columbia. (Indeed, British Columbia made the building
of the railway by 1881 a condition of its entry into Confederation.)
A country cut off from its constituent parts by rivers, mountain ranges,

and thousands of miles of uninhabited prairies was easy prey for the land hunger of the Yankee. The strength of the nation, so the argument went, depended upon its ability to unite all its parts into a viable unit. In a country as vast as Canada communication links between the east and west were the necessary foundations of nationhood. A railway, a transcontinental railway at that, would provide those essential communication links.

For the people of Canada the construction of the CPR would have both immediate and long-term effects. In the first place, the actual building of the line gave employment to thousands of workers. First there were the survey crews whose reports were essential for choosing not only the most direct route but also the easiest route, both in terms of the time required for construction and of the ultimate safety and durability of the track. Once a particular route had been selected, huge armies of graders and scrapers arrived on the scene. To them fell the task of preparing the route for the laying of track. These men cleared trees and bush, filled in swamps and gulleys, and dynamited some of the hardest rock in the world. Once the ground was fairly level and free from obstructions, tracklaying crews moved in.

Every rail and every tie was laid by hand over the thousands of miles between Ontario and the Pacific shore. A spiking gang followed closely behind to drive the heavy iron spikes into the rails. Through late spring and summer all the men, regardless of their particular job, faced a common enemy. Huge mosquitoes, 'which in size and appearance might have been mistaken for a cross between a bull dog and a housefly', made the men miserable by day and by night.

The surveyors for the CPR faced the extreme hardships of both isolation and monotony. They travelled to their place of work by canoe when possible, but for the most part were forced to walk. It was not uncommon for the surveyors and later for the construction crews to find themselves hundreds of miles from the nearest town. In addition to being cut off from the outside world, the workers also had to cope with the perils of both the climate and the construction.

Marcus Smith, who worked on the Rocky Mountain stretch, faced dangers that would have compelled a less stout-hearted man to find other employment. 'Once,' he wrote, 'my mule fell with me from a cliff into deep water from which I narrowly escaped drowning; again while climbing a steep mountain side a mass of loose rock and earth began to move, carrying me down within fifty feet of a precipice 600 feet high.' J. E. Secretan, who began working for the company while still a very young man, recalled the depressing monotony of his work on the section north of Lake Superior. 'Wading knee-deep through muskegs all day and fighting mosquitoes all night, and living on salt pork ... and beans, with dried apples for dessert, was our daily routine.'

Secretan was later to find his work in British Columbia more interesting, though hardly less difficult. There much of the area where he was working had been subject to forest fires, and as a consequence preparing it for tracklaying was somewhat easier. The main problem, however, was the swamps. They had to be bridged in one manner or another so that the surveyors, along with their mules and supplies, could continue their work. Secretan tried to overcome this problem by building a

sort of 'Courduroy' [road] with four logs abreast laid longitudinally and securely pinned down, but soon discovered that the mentality of the pack-mule did not rise to this elaborate causeway. He or she invariably preferred to walk on one or the other of the outside logs, and were sometimes successful, but if not they went over into the swamp, pack and all (about 200 to 250 pounds) and so delayed the rest of the proceedings until we dug them out.

The spirit of these surveyors who endured so much in determining the route for the CPR is perhaps illustrated by the singing that went on each night as they sat around campfires in the Fraser Valley or north of the shores of Lake Superior.

> *Far away from those we love dearest*
> *Who long and wish for home,*
> *The thought of whom each lone heart cheereth*
> *As 'mid these North West wilds we roam*
> *Yet still each one performs his duty*
> *And gaily sings. . . .*

Once the surveyors had completed their task, the graders, track-layers, and spiking gangs were close on their heels. Chinese, Indians,

A five-mile loop of track.
Find out approximately how long the track from
Calgary to Vancouver is.
What is the distance 'as the crow flies'?

Americans, Swedes, Irishmen, Englishmen, Scots, Italians, and Canadians worked hand in hand to complete the CPR. Their task was no
less hazardous than that of the surveyors who had preceded them.
'Texas', who worked on a construction gang in the Kicking Horse Pass,
complained that he 'never felt safe, for every minute or so would come
the cry: Look out below! or Stand from under! and a heavy stone or
rock would come thundering down the slope right amongst us.' The
work was so dangerous that there are some who claim that 'every mile
of tunnel and track was sealed with the blood of men' along the British
Columbia section of the line.

Texas and his fellow workers across the country did everything from
smoothing slopes and building stone walls at the bottom of embank-
ments to blasting rock with deadly nitroglycerine. Work with this

95

A track through the Selkirk Mountains.
What is the steepest gradient that can be used by a
modern train? Has this changed from the time the
CPR was first built?

chemical was particularly dangerous because it exploded with the
slightest movement or with a dip in the temperature. Because it was
so unstable and the roads were either non-existent or terribly uneven,
nitroglycerine could not be safely transported by wagon. Instead, the
highly volatile chemical was placed in bottles, wrapped in protective
cloth, packed into canvas packs and strapped to men's backs. To
stumble or fall meant certain death for the carrier and those around
him.

96

Sometimes the lethal bottles leaked onto the rocks or into the ground as the chemical was transported from place to place. Any unsuspecting crew member or pack animal that inadvertently stepped on one of these 'spots' was immediately blown up. The risks entailed while working with nitroglycerine were accentuated by the fact that not all of the workers spoke or even understood basic English. As a result some died needlessly simply because they had not understood the dangers involved. On other occasions too much nitro was used in blasting and those who were perched too close to the scene of the explosion were immediately killed.

In the desolate area north of Lake Superior nitroglycerine was used daily to blast some of the toughest rock formations in Canada. The results were often disastrous. In one fifty-mile stretch of track, it is said that more than thirty men lost their lives. All this was only part of the price paid in building a transcontinental railway.

Who were these men who so willingly risked their lives? More than one journalist described them as 'the scum and offscourings of the filthiest slums' of the world. Others described them simply as adventurers who sought freedom from the cares of a humdrum world. Perhaps it is best to let these men describe themselves. In one of the many songs that were sung to pass the evening hours away the workers themselves recognized the different forces that had brought them to the construction camps of Canada.

> For some of us are tramps, for whom work has no charms,
> And some of us are Farmers, aworking for our farms,
> But all are jolly fellows who came from near and far,
> To work up in the Rockies of the CPR.

Much of the labour that went into the British Columbia section of the railroad was performed by Chinese workers. Some had apparently immigrated to Canada from California at the height of the gold rush of 1858 and had stayed on. The others came directly from South China to work on the Canadian railroad. These latter were most often hired in large numbers by the CPR contractors through agencies in Kwang Tung province. These agencies assumed all responsibility for the transportation of the workers to Canada and for their contracts with the Canadian companies. In return for this service the agencies were

Railway accidents. Top: Tracks washed out by
heavy rains, near Dundas, Ont., in 1859. Below:
Broken axle-tree, near Georgetown, Ont., in 1864.

paid about two per cent of the worker's yearly salary. They were also
reimbursed by the individual worker for the cost of the fare to Canada.
This debt usually amounted to something in the neighbourhood of
forty dollars.

For these workers there was only one goal. They wanted to save
enough money to return to China and buy a small plot of land for
themselves and their families. Since they were accustomed to wages

of less than ten cents a day in their native China, they fell easy prey to unscrupulous employers in this country. The Chinese, for example, earned about one dollar a day while those of other nationalities who did precisely the same work were paid double that amount. In addition, the contractors insisted that the Chinese workers purchase their work clothes and other necessities from the company store at somewhat inflated prices. Failure to comply with this request resulted in a wage reduction of sometimes as much as twenty cents a day.

To make matters worse, there is evidence to suggest that deaths resulting from accidents appeared to occur more frequently among Chinese work gangs. In one case a supervisor failed to warn his Chinese workers of an impending explosion. His oversight caused at least one death and almost resulted in a riot. On other occasions it seemed as though the Chinese were given the most dangerous assignments because they were considered 'less human' than the other workers. Some British Columbia newspapers, for example, neglected to report the deaths of Chinese workers, although they never failed to record the fate of others who died during the construction of the CPR.

Sickness also took a high toll among the Chinese. This was in part due to their basic diet, which usually consisted of rice and stale ground salmon. In many cases it led to scurvy and eventual death. The climate, too, seemed to undermine the health of many of these workers.

Despite the very real risks of disease, injury, or even death, the Chinese continued to look to railroad construction for employment. Few realized that even the hardest working among them would never make a 'fortune'. Simple arithmetic clearly shows the impossibility of the Chinese worker's goal. In the first place, there were almost three months in the year when winter made work impossible and as a result no money was earned. Even though the Chinese labourer received about twenty-five dollars a month for the other nine months, he had many expenses to pay. Work clothes, for example, cost as much as one hundred dollars a year. Then, of course, money had to be found for accommodation, tools, and medical expenses. As if this was not enough, there was still the initial debt of some forty dollars in transportation costs that had to be repaid to the Kwang Tung agent.

Once construction on the CPR was completed the Chinese were left

99

Winnipeg, 1875.
Compare this view with the following picture.

to fend for themselves. With only a few hard-earned dollars in a country that did not want them as permanent residents, Chinese labourers faced a grim future. The dream of returning one day to Kwang Tung was never realized by many of them. The unhappy fate of the Chinese who worked so hard, and often paid for the privilege with their lives, is one of the most tragic chapters in the building of the Canadian Pacific.

The Chinese, however, were not the only ones who helped to build the railway, nor were they the only men who died in the course of its construction. The others who came to work on the CPR were usually hired through the many newspaper advertisements that appeared in cities across North America and Europe. They came because the wages were good and the promise of adventure was real. Some hoped to save enough money to purchase farmland in western Canada. Some wanted to take their savings and return one day to their birthplace in England, Europe, or the United States. Others were content merely to enjoy the fun and friendship of the work camps and let the future take care of itself. And undoubtedly there were some who sought refuge from a bad marriage, a criminal past, or a business failure in the isolation and anonymity of the construction gang. Far from news of the outside world, they worked at a steady pace to link the rails from east to west.

Winnipeg, 1880.
*How many of these buildings do you think had
been erected since 1875?*

As construction proceeded across the sparsely inhabited northern half of the continent, it brought about fundamental changes in the lifestyle of the people. More than one farmer cheerfully confirmed that a railway adds 25 per cent to the value of every farm within fifty miles of it, doubles the value of those nearer than that, and quadruples the value of farms through which it passes.

The rapid increase in the value of land invariably led to certain abuses that were difficult if not impossible to control. Many honest but simple men were cheated by a few unscrupulous land speculators. Sometimes the settlers had little understanding of the great worth of their property. There is a story often told of a young English farmer who bought a hundred and sixty acres of land in what seemed to him the middle of nowhere. A year after settling in the area the young man decided to return to his native land. The farmer eagerly accepted the first offer to come his way. In return for the land he received three pairs of socks, a second-hand musical instrument, a few packages of cigarettes, eighteen dollars in cash, and a ticket to Liverpool, England. The new owner quickly turned around and sold this same parcel of land to someone else for eighty thousand dollars. Everyone but the young farmer seemed to know that the area was destined to become the town of Brandon, Manitoba.

101

CPR yards, Winnipeg.
Why has Winnipeg developed as an important railway city?

As the railway snaked its way across the West it transformed villages into thriving towns. Winnipeg was described in 1873 as a muddy, disreputable village. Without sidewalks or pavement, life was a constant struggle against the thick gluey gumbo of the streets. The arrival of the CPR made Winnipeg the 'Gateway to the West' and an important distributing centre for the east-west flow of manufactured goods and farm produce. In little more than ten years visitors to the now booming town marvelled at the splendid buildings and the huge plate-glass windows of the stores that lined Main Street. The narrow, muddy laneways were now wide, pleasant streets. Even more impressive were

102

The arrival of the first train in Vancouver, 1887.
*What factors made the railway as important in the
growth of Vancouver as it was in the growth of
Winnipeg?*

the lights that illuminated all the major roads after dark. Winnipeg
had certainly come a long way.

The arrival of the railway also gave rise to towns where none had
existed before. Secretan recounts an interesting tale about the birth of
Brandon. According to him the CPR was looking for a good location to
set up the first divisional point west of Winnipeg. Here the company
would eventually build storage shops and machine sheds. The search
for the ideal location took some time. At last company officials were
convinced of the suitability of a particular parcel of land. The owner
of the land was contacted and immediately offered fifty thousand dollars
for his property. The farmer was delighted at the prospect of so much
money. In fact it was really hard for him to imagine just how much
money that was. The deal might have been agreeably settled right then
and there had it not been for the farmer's well-meaning friends and

neighbours. If the land was worth fifty thousand, maybe it was really worth much more, they reasoned. At length the farmer was persuaded to demand another ten thousand. The company refused to meet the farmer's demand, the divisional point was moved a few miles west of the original site, and the farmer was left with his farm and his financially astute advisors to console him. This divisional point became the centre around which the town of Brandon came to life.

Greed, it seems, proved to be the undoing of more than one land-owner who attempted to drive an unreasonably hard bargain with Canadian Pacific officials. The city of Calgary, for example, was originally located on the eastern bank of the Elbow River. An enter-prising group of men bought a hundred acres of land in the area, surveyed it, and then sold 'future' town lots to a long line of waiting buyers. Canadian Pacific officials and this group of businessmen disagreed about the value of the property on which a proposed station was to be built. Negotiations proved futile for both parties. What would the company do? In the end the CPR built a station on the west side of the river. As a result settlers and shopkeepers were attracted to the general area of the station and the businessmen lost their investment. The little town that grew up later became the city of Calgary—much to the sorrow of the businessmen who had gambled and lost.

One by one the obstacles confronting the Canadian Pacific Railway were overcome by the daring and courage not only of company officials but also of the unnamed men who worked under the most trying physical conditions. On November 7, 1885, the great project was completed. Donald Smith, a director of the company, had the honour of driving the last iron spike into the ground at Craigellachie, B.C., where the track laid from Vancouver met the line coming from Montreal. It was especially fitting that the last spike, like all the other spikes used in the construction of the Canadian Pacific, was made of iron. For iron perhaps best symbolizes the strength of purpose and execution that made the dream of a transcontinental railway a reality. Once the last spike was driven home, enthusiastic cheers echoed from the small crowd of officials and workmen who had gathered for the simple ceremony.

Major General Sam Steele was one of the first to make the journey

The colonist car.
*In what ways was the accommodation for passengers
superior to that described in the previous chapter?*

from Craigellachie to Vancouver on the newly completed transcontinental railroad. The small train flew along the tracks at the
outrageous speed of fifty-seven miles an hour, 'roaring in and out of
the tunnels and whirling around the curves' high in the Rocky
Mountains. In one nineteen-mile stretch of rail there were thirteen
tunnels and snow sheds. The snow sheds were really a safety device.
They were built along the side of the mountains and had sloping roofs
to protect the tracks from possible avalanches. Major Steele, like the
others who rode the train that day, was impressed by the skill and
courage of the surveyors, engineers, and workers who had braved the
climate and the topography of the Rocky Mountain section to bring

New Advertisements.

STEAM TO CARIBOO !

The British Columbia
GENERAL TRANSPORTATION COMPANY

Will place Four of **THOMSON'S PATENT ROAD STEAM-ERS** on the route between **Yale** and **Barkerville** in the First Week in April, and will be prepared to enter into Contracts for the conveyance of Freight from **Yale** to **Soda Creek** in EIGHT DAYS. Through Contracts will be made as soon as the condition of the road above Quesnelmouth permits.

Rates of Passage will be advertised in due time.

BARNARD & BEEDY, Managers.

OFFCE—Yates Street, next door to Wells, Fargo & Co.'s

Railway or streetcar?
Why did road steamers not survive as a method of
transportation?

106

the Canadian Pacific to its western terminus at the Pacific. Though Steele was most likely unaware of it, his safety and comfort were ensured by the dedicated groups of men who formed track patrols to inspect the line for fallen boulders or a slide of snow that could spell trouble for the approaching train. Nothing was left to chance.

Lady Macdonald, wife of the Prime Minister of the day, made her first excursion with her husband across the nation by train in July 1886. As a mark of her great confidence in the safety of the line, she travelled over part of the Rocky Mountain stretch on the cow catcher. The cow catcher was a frame of timber attached to the lower front end of the engine. It was constructed in a simple basket-like form in order to push away any obstacles that might be on the track and prevent a possible derailment. To ride through the dizzying heights of the Rockies in such a manner would take more than a little courage.

The first regular passenger train arrived in Vancouver on Tuesday, May 23, 1887. The engine made a splendid impression on all who saw it. Its brass work shone like the purest gold and the steel trim was polished as brightly as possible. Flags, evergreens, and shields bearing the words Montreal and Vancouver added further decoration to the engine. A local newspaper described the happy scene as the first regular train entered the station and pulled up in Vancouver.

The scene for a few minutes was indescribable, shaking of hands and congratulations were the order of the day and everyone seemed delighted beyond expression. . . . About this time the music of the band was heard and a moment later a procession of several hundred people headed by the City Band and Fire Brigade in full dress came marching down the roadway and halted at the station.

Mayor McLean smiled with pride as he mounted the platform and in a booming voice proposed three cheers for the CPR.

The first train consisted of a baggage car, a colonist car, a first-class day car and sleeper, and the drawingroom or dining car. Of all these it was the colonist car that was to become the most important in the history of the Canadian Pacific. It would one day take credit for transporting almost a million European immigrants to the open and relatively unsettled Prairies of western Canada. But this contribution to Canadian development belonged to the future.

The jubilation that surrounded the arrival of the first train in Vancouver was repeated in 1945 when the CPR gave that first engine '374' to the citizens of Vancouver. It was renovated and then decorated much as it had been in 1887. As in 1887, the day chosen for the ceremonious re-enactment of its first arrival was a beautiful one. 'Spectators crowded the station platform; more looked down from tall office building windows and the dock railings; every point of vantage was packed.' Everyone wanted to see '374' break through the wide blue ribbon that spanned the track just as it had done some fifty-eight years ago. A pandemonium of cheers and whistles from the steamships in the harbour broke loose, cameras snapped, and all was smiles and congratulations. To add authenticity to the occasion many dressed as in the early days. There were speeches and luncheons much the same as on that day in 1887.

The everyday running of the Canadian Pacific was certainly not as much fun as the arrival of that first train. One of the most interesting problems faced by the company, though, was that of security. Encouraged by their successes south of the border, one notorious gang of robbers decided to try their luck in Canada. The feared and ruthless Bill Miner was the unquestioned leader of the trio. He was assisted by two other gunmen, 'Shorty' Coloquhous and Billy Dunn. As the train approached the Kamloops station, the robbers attacked. They managed to get away with some money, though the exact amount was never really determined. Without any further fuss, the gang mounted their horses and headed out in a southerly direction. Commissioner Perry of the Mounted Police quickly organized a posse of volunteers to track down the desperadoes.

Everything seemed to be against the forces of law and order. The weather was poor and the visibility dreadful. To make matters worse the horses seemed to be tiring with the strain. Despite these obstacles the posse pressed on for almost forty-eight hours before they spotted the gang. A short, sharp gun fight took place, but the Mounted Police successfully captured Miner and his companions in crime. The speed with which the culprits were apprehended served as an important warning for others who may have considered the possibility of robbing the Canadian Pacific Railway.

Far less interesting, but no doubt of greater importance to some Canadians, was the high cost of freight transportation by rail. Few had the time, the money, or even the inclination to travel as passengers across Canada. Those who lived in the West were particularly hard hit by the high costs. They resented the fact that manufactured goods cost in some cases twice as much in Calgary as in Toronto. Despite their protests, in the main their demands were simply ignored. One day, though, when the hundreds of thousands of European immigrants were settled in the Prairies, the voice of the West would be strong. And then the Canadian Pacific and Canada itself would be forced to take notice.

7 Carts and Boats

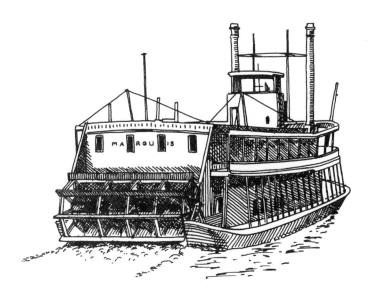

After the construction of the Canadian Pacific Railway, the ordeal of settlers in the West was far less severe than it had been for early settlers in both eastern and western Canada. The CPR made the journey from the point of arrival in Canada far less arduous than it had formerly been, and those who chose to settle in the treeless part of the Prairies were not confronted with the difficult task of clearing the land. For those who arrived in the West before the CPR, though, conditions were not as favourable. These early settlers faced many of the problems that had confronted pioneers in Ontario, Québec, and the Atlantic provinces.

The first major settlement west of Ontario was the Red River Colony, situated near what is now Winnipeg, Manitoba. Between the years 1811 and 1815, Lord Selkirk, a Scotsman concerned about poverty in Britain, transported 300 men, women, and children from the Scottish Highlands and from the north of Ireland to the new colony. Life was not easy for these pioneers. The usual hazards of trans-Atlantic transport were compounded by the particular sea route these settlers took to Canada. They did not follow the St Lawrence as thousands before them had done. Rather they entered Canada through the icy opening of Hudson Bay. From there they travelled the network of rivers that eventually led them south to the site of the new colony. To the

110

York boats rigged with sails.
*What advantages and disadvantages did the York
boat have when compared with the canoe?*

usual perils of transportation in Canada were added the effects of the
sub-Arctic climate.

In 1812, for example, a group of fever-stricken settlers from the
parish of Kildonan in Scotland reached the northern port of Churchill
in what is now Manitoba. In order to reach the Red River Colony, they
had to get to York Factory, which is at the mouth of the network of
rivers that would take them south. But the captain of their ship
refused to take them there. As a consequence, the party of 83 was
compelled to spend the winter along the Arctic banks of the Churchill
River and then, in the spring, to walk overland to York Factory. From
there canoes and York boats would take the settlers to their destination.

York boats, which were crucial in the trading activities of the
Hudson's Bay Company, were characterized by a traveller as 'long,
broad, and heavy'. They were capable of carrying 'forty hundredweight,
and nine men, besides three or four passengers, with provisions for
themselves and the crews'. Despite the great weight transported by
these vehicles, it was estimated that they did not 'draw more than three
feet of water when loaded' and were very light for their size. Usually
each boat was manned by eight to twelve voyageurs, although thirty

111

A Red River cart.
Why did these carts have such large wheels?

men were required to portage each boat. When it became necessary to carry a York boat around rapids or shallow water, the crews of all boats in the 'brigade'—usually a number of these boats travelled together—would portage the boats, one at a time.

Perhaps the fertile soils of the Red River Colony made the effort of the journey in these boats from Hudson Bay worthwhile, although difficulties were not to end with arrival at the new settlement. It was not long before the Scottish and Irish settlers came to a bloody clash with those of French-Indian background. The Métis, as they were called, had been convinced by the North West Company that they must resist the encroachments of the colonists because the animals of the plains, especially the buffalo, would move far away from the settlements. In addition, some settlers became disenchanted and eventually left the fledgling colony. But despite these setbacks, the colony survived.

The chief mode of overland transport in the early years of settlement in the West was a vehicle called the Red River Cart, an adaptation of a Scottish cart to Canadian circumstances. These carts comprised a light, box-like body that was placed on a single axle with six-foot-high wheels. The entire structure was held together by strands of buffalo hide—not one nail was used. The outstanding characteristic of these

112

carts was the deafening squeaks emitted from their wheels. The axles were not greased because dust from the prairies would soon prevent the wheels from turning. It is no wonder that some Westerners referred to the Red River Cart as the 'North West Fiddle'.

These carts, which frequently travelled in brigades across the Prairies, left deep ruts in the soil. Soon the routes taken by these brigades became the main thoroughfares of the West and even today underlie some streets of prairie towns and cities. They would also dictate the route of the Canadian National Railway (CNR).

A second important group of settlers who arrived in the Canadian West before the construction of the CPR were Mennonites from Russia. While the hope of an improvement in their standard of living may have been the primary consideration underlying the Scottish and Irish settlement along the Red River, the appeal for the Mennonites was the promise of religious freedom in the Canadian West. In their native Russia they were increasingly subject to Tsarist laws that they felt compromised their religious beliefs. In the Canadian West they had government assurances that they would be left to practise their religion as they saw fit.

As a consequence, between the years 1873-76 over six thousand Mennonites were transported from southern Russia to Manitoba. Their journey was less arduous than that of many other settlers because, first of all, the Mennonites had been skilful farmers in Russia—the type of settler Canada needed—and they were consequently able to afford comparatively reasonable accommodations on the long trip across the ocean. They were not compelled to travel 'steerage', spending days below the decks of a ship. Moreover, once they arrived in Canada, for many the shock of encountering new and strange customs was offset by the presence of Mennonites who had immigrated to Waterloo, Ontario, some years before. Many Mennonites spent their first winter with this group and were able to earn some money by working as farm hands. More important, they were able to familiarize themselves with Canadian customs. Most immigrants to Canada during these and later years would not be so fortunate as to have someone to acquaint them with Canadian ways. In addition, many would not have the security provided by settling in groups as the Mennonites did. They would be left to

113

The arrival of the first Mennonites in Winnipeg, 1874.
Why have the Mennonites been such successful farmers?
Where are the Mennonite farms located in the West
today? What problems are they having today? Why?

A train of covered carts bringing settlers to the West. *Why did these settlers travel in groups? Was it for the same reasons as the voyageurs travelled in brigades of canoes?*

their own resources in making their way in a strange and often hostile new land.

Before the CPR was completed, the usual route from Ontario to the West was through the United States. The reason for this was simple. The Canadian Shield posed a formidable barrier even to the most hardy of travellers. The Canadian government, however, was fearful that if settlers went West via the United States, they would be lured by the promise of a better life south of the border and would never complete their journey to the great unfilled expanse of Canada between Ontario and the Rocky Mountains. Consequently, settlers were required to reach the Prairies over the Dawson Trail that connected Manitoba and Ontario by a network of wagon trails and lakes.

Travel over the Dawson Trail required first of all a 96-mile rail journey from Toronto to Collingwood, on the shores of Georgian Bay. Then there was a 532-mile journey by steamer to Fort William on Lake Superior. From Fort William the traveller went another 45 miles by wagon to Shebandowan Lake, where he was given passage in an open boat for the 310-mile voyage to the Lake of the Woods. From the Lake of the Woods it was another 95 miles by wagon to Fort Garry (now Winnipeg).

Upon completion of this arduous trip one weary traveller complained to Donald Smith, who was later to become a director of the CPR:

Ain't I a healthy sight? I've come by the government water route

115

from Thunder Bay, and its taken me twenty-five days to do it. During that time I've been half-starved. . . . The water used to pour into my bunk at nights, and the boat was so leaky that every bit of baggage I've got is water-logged and ruined. I've broke my arm and sprained my ankle helping to carry half a dozen trunks over a dozen portages, and when I refused to take a paddle on one of the boats, an Ottawa Irishman told me to. . . , and said that if I gave him anymore of my . . . chat he'd let me get off and walk to Winnipeg.

While this route may have been cheaper than going through the United States, the Mennonites were reluctant to travel across the Dawson Trail, and after some protest they were finally given permission by the Canadian government to enter the Canadian West via the United States. Once the Mennonites reached their destination, it was not long before their farms became models of what could be done through hard work and dedication.

During the nineteenth century settlers from the older parts of Canada and settlers from Europe trickled into the Canadian West, but it was not until the turn of the century that the trickle became a flood. If the prairie schooner or covered wagon symbolizes the settlement of the American West, the steam engine is the vehicle that best represents the experience of those hundreds of thousands of people who established new homes in the Canadian West at the turn of the century. Not only did it provide a vital life link between east and west, but also it provided a means whereby settlers from older parts of Canada and Europe could reach the fertile region of what is now Manitoba, Saskatchewan, and Alberta.

The Canadian government, for a number of reasons, embarked on a massive program of encouraging immigration. Government agents travelled to European cities to advertise the advantages of the Canadian West. In this endeavour they were often assisted by private steamship companies who hoped to create profits for themselves by encouraging immigration. The picture they painted of Canada was so attractive that one later settler remarked that Canada 'looked very inviting when one studied the pictures of a lean, handsome young man on horseback, dressed like a cowboy, waving good-bye to his pretty wife, who stood on the verandah of a charming house.' That Canada was a promised

116

Settlers arriving in the West by railway.
*From what parts of the world might these settlers
have come?*

land was never doubted by those who were attracted by the advertising
of government agencies and private companies. 'All fiction, when
Canada was mentioned,' the same immigrant wrote, 'invariably spoke
of cattle kings and wheat growers who owned thousands of acres and
returned for long holidays to the land of their birth; and while the
government pamphlets did not exactly promise this to the settler of
the right sort, they certainly did nothing to deny it.'

A second way that the government encouraged immigration to
Canada was by giving bonuses to ticket agents who persuaded immigrants to go to Canada rather than elsewhere. For every person over

eighteen who bought a ticket to Canada, the ticket agent received $4.86. For every person under eighteen, he received $2.43. These were no small amounts, given turn-of-the-century prices! There were, however, limitations to this generous bonus system. The opening of the Canadian West meant opportunities for farmers and railway workers, and people who would work in these occupations were most sought after. While British immigrants were 'preferred', consideration was also given to immigrants who would fill these occupations from France, Belgium, Holland, Denmark, Norway, Sweden, Germany, and Finland. Immigrants from other countries were considered 'less desirable' than these groups and no bonuses were given for selling them tickets.

In addition to these factors—which explain, to some extent, the flood of immigration to Canada at the turn of the century—it is also important to appreciate that events in Europe had prompted people to look elsewhere for a place to live. Hard times and social unrest were sufficient to prompt numerous Poles, Hungarians, Russians, Lithuanians, Italians, Greeks, and Roumanians to consider life in Canada. They were attracted not only by the prospect of cheap land but by the chance to escape from political tyranny.

Of less importance but of comparable interest are the activities of benevolent societies in promoting immigration to Canada during this period. In England such agencies as the Salvation Army and numerous other charitable organizations were assisting unfortunates with their passage money and with getting a start in Canada. Unlike England, where industrialization had resulted in poverty for millions of urban residents, Canada was felt to be a land of unlimited opportunity. Perhaps the words of one English immigrant best express the optimism of thousands of others like him who made the journey to Canada.

Why have I come to Canada? Well that is easy. To get work. I haven't earned a penny since Christmas. I have walked twenty miles a day looking for a job. For every position that is open there are hundreds of applicants. They actually have to call out the police. I have been in one position twenty-eight years looking after the stud of a wealthy man. The governor died. The stables were sold. Every man of us was discharged; some there forty years, too. It was tough, I can tell you. I have been looking for work ever since.

118

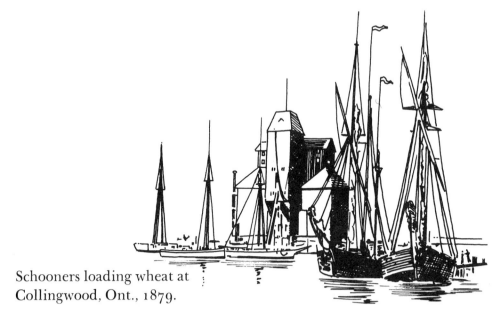

Schooners loading wheat at Collingwood, Ont., 1879.

A second group who, it was hoped, would find a better life in Canada were the thousands of English orphans, boys and girls, who were shipped from the orphanages and work houses of English cities. These children took up occupations in countless industries—there was no child employment legislation at that time—although the largest single group who requested English orphans were young recently married farmers who could not afford to hire an adult labourer, elderly farmers whose grown children had moved elsewhere, and owners of large farms who kept a number of men yet required a few boys to do odd jobs. While the lot of children working in these circumstances may not have been the best, it could not have been worse than that of children who remained in institutions in England.

Despite the fact that the Canadian government tried to encourage the settlement of Englishmen in the farming areas of the West, it soon became apparent that life in English cities did not prepare the Englishman for the harsh life of the farm. So ill-prepared were the majority of English immigrants for this type of life that it was not long before Western farmers, when advertising for farm labourers, included the stipulation that 'no Englishman need apply'. The effects of urban poverty on Englishmen are also reflected in deportation figures. By far the majority of those who were found to be medically unfit for entry into Canada were English. For the period 1901 to 1909, one out of every 218 British immigrants was, for medical reasons, deported to England. Of immigrants coming from the rest of Europe, only one in every 474 immigrants was deported—a sizeable difference.

Immigrants who perhaps best met the requirements of the Canadian government were those from the United States. Not only were these people found to be good farmers, but they were also used to the hardships encountered on the Canadian frontier. The 'Last Best West', as the Canadian West was referred to during the early twentieth century, offered the last opportunity to those from the United States who wished to acquire cheap, good land for farming. The American 'wild west', with its legendary cattle drives, free land, and Indian wars, had long been tamed when the Canadian Prairies were only being opened to settlement.

While immigrants from England, Germany, Holland, the Ukraine, Poland, Russia, Ireland, Scotland, and Greece may have come to Canada for different reasons, once they arrived at Halifax, Québec, or Montreal, the majority shared similar experiences in reaching their final destination. A Canadian clergyman described what happened to people from the time they disembarked until they finally reached their new prairie homes.

First comes the medical examination. Then all must pass through the 'cattle pen'—a series of iron-barred rooms and passage ways. They must go in single file, and each pass before various officials who question them as to their nationality and destination, and the amount of money they have in their possession. All this is very necessary, but it is a weary anxious time. No one can tell what will come next. Many feel that they will be stopped. Some are turned back—one taken and the others left. Now, there is a customs examination. At first tickets are arranged for, baggage transferred, and the immigrants find themselves bundled into a colonist car. This is another new experience—not altogether a pleasant one either, since they are not accustomed to cooking and sleeping in such small quarters. Some have not made proper provision. After several days, all are glad to get off the train at one of the large

120

A Galician homestead.

distributing points. Here again are the government officials who arrange everything. Within a few days they are sent out on some new branch line, and with their belongings are set down at a little 'siding' on the prairie. They have some friends perhaps who drive them to their homestead, or who shelter them for a few weeks. Now begins the new life in the strange land.

Journeys such as this were often uneventful, but there were some that involved distressing experiences. A story is told of a Polish family who, upon arrival, was informed that one child had weak eyes:

Of course, she must be deported. But do we think what it means— the shock to the family when they learn that their little one is to be sent back and they are to go on. Gladly they, too, would return, but they have no money. The poor have no choice. In spite of the father's and mother's grief the little girl is taken from them.

Fortunately not all setbacks on the journey were as heart-breaking as this incident. For example,

One day an immigrant train was brought to a sudden stop by an alarm from a Galician family that they had lost one of their children, a boy of eight, who had tumbled out of the window. All was interest and excitement, and the parents were loud in their expressions of dismay and grief, but as the train went slowly backward the young hopeful was discovered walking along the track and was finally picked

A prairie log and mud house, 1907.
*Compare this house with those of the settlers in
Upper Canada. What differences are there?*

*up, quite unhurt, on perceiving which the parents experienced a
sudden revulsion of feeling, and gave their offspring a vigorous whip-
ping for the trouble he had caused by his escapade.*

It should not be assumed that all was well for those who finally
reached their destination safely. More than one immigrant was
disappointed when he realized that land was not as cheap as he had
been led to believe, or that the best land was already taken. In cases
such as these, no option was available to the immigrant but to find work
either as a farm labourer or in one of the towns or cities that were
sprouting up across the Prairies. In many cases immigrants never got
beyond cities like Winnipeg, which they had originally hoped would
merely be temporary stop-overs on the way to a life of prosperous
farming. Their lot was to provide labour for the emerging industrial
enterprises of the day. Indeed, despite the fact that the Canadian
government was primarily concerned with promoting rural settlement,
the vast majority of immigrants eventually took up residence in towns
and cities.

A prairie sod hut.
Settlers in the Prairies encountered certain
difficulties because of the nature of the terrain.
What were they, and how were they different from
the problems of Upper Canada farmers?

For these people life was hard. Poor wages, inadequate housing, and overcrowding, along with an absence of services like Medicare, which we now take for granted, combined to make the lives of immigrants and the native urban poor barely tolerable. Under such conditions alcoholism was common and crime was rife; children were compelled to stop school in order to contribute to the family income; and it was not uncommon for families to break up completely.

The exact nature of conditions in which some immigrants were forced to live is provided by the following account of a 'home' given by a Mission worker.

A small room at the back, very crowded, with double bed, small stove and table. The air was very, very bad and both door and window were kept tightly closed. Father was out looking for work. The mother was out washing. The stove was dirty and piled up with dirty pots and kettles. The table showed signs of breakfast—dirty granite dishes and spoons ... and part of a loaf of bread from which the cat was now having its breakfast.

The bed was like all the beds in this class of home—mattress covered by an old gray blanket, two big, dirty-looking pillows and some old clothes. This was the children's playground, for there was no floor space uncovered. Under the bed we noticed some cooking utensils, white-wash brush, and axe, spade, a dozen or more empty bottles, some clothing and a sack of bread.

Such sights, it seems, were not uncommon in Canadian cities.

For those immigrants who did manage to acquire a farm, life was not easy, but it was far better than the life of the city dweller. The hours of toil may have been long but the food was nourishing and the air was clean. Like early settlers in the East, the western farmer also lived in a house made of logs when trees were available. Where trees were not in supply, houses of prairie sod were a common sight. Plaster for the inside of the log houses was made by mixing clay and water. Homemade wooden furniture as well as spinning wheels were often found in dwellings such as this. For the early settler, 'store-bought' furniture and clothes that could be shipped by rail from the East were a luxury rather than a necessity. Articles such as these were not as important as a good team of horses or a plough.

Life on the Prairies was lonely. Miles of open country separated one farm from another. Often children would walk for miles from their homes to one-room school houses. Before the invention and use of radio, primary contacts with the outside world were maintained through books, magazines, and newspapers, and through the inevitable gossip after church on a Sunday.

Once the successful immigrant arrived in the West and established himself on his farm, his reliance on the CPR did not come to an end; in fact, as was the case with his Canadian-born neighbour, it increased. The farmer now had to get his crop to market. How else could he do this but by rail? All of the rivers and streams of the West, even if they had been navigable, could not have handled the agricultural bounty of the Prairies. To have shipped produce overland by wagon would have been slow, inefficient, and costly. The Canadian Pacific Railway was the only answer.

8 Cars and Bicycles

In the days when urban centres were small and when foot, cart, and buggy were the principal means of transport, everybody who worked in the city lived in the city; residential quarters and commercial premises existed side by side and all classes of the population intermingled. It was still possible to walk to work, to church, and to all forms of entertainment.

Horse-drawn streetcars that ran along tracks were first introduced in Toronto in 1861. The cars were completely open and passengers were exposed to all extremes of weather. The wooden cars were almost sixteen feet in length and had an open platform at each end. Passengers were free to enter the car from either the back or the front. The driver sat in the open without protection from the cold except for a wooden box filled with straw that was supposed to keep his feet warm. He stopped anywhere along the track to pick up passengers, and upon occasion a car would wait for someone to finish a hurried breakfast. In Montreal the horse cars would stop and wait while passengers completed their shopping or paid short calls on friends. No tickets were used at first, and since passengers could enter and leave at both ends of the car, many people avoided paying fares altogether. To stop the car, passengers pulled a string that was attached to the driver's foot. Later, buzzers were installed for this purpose.

A horse-drawn streetcar.
*What improvements have been made in this streetcar
compared with the earliest one described in the text?*

When the first horse-drawn car made its initial run in Toronto the car ran off the tracks, but the passengers soon had it back in place. 'This occurred several times,' reported the *Globe*, 'but the passengers treated the delay as a joke and the crowd were always ready to give a shove or a lift to keep it moving.' Later in the year a street railway was opened from Yonge and Queen Streets to the west end of the city. 'The cars were gaily decorated with flags,' reported one of the local newspapers, 'and although the novelty of a street railway has to a great extent worn off, the sidewalks were crowded with spectators as the cars passed along.'

The horses that pulled the heavy cars in summer and winter worked long hours, and although the pace was generally slow the loads were usually heavy, especially in the wintertime when the cars had to be pulled through the snow-filled streets. It is not surprising that after only one year of employment the tired horses had to be retired from active duty. Replacements, though, were always easy to find.

In winter the presence of the street railway caused a considerable amount of friction between its employees and the storekeepers along Yonge Street. During heavy snowfalls the horse-drawn cars carried

A streetcar fitted with runners.
*Throughout this book difficulties for travellers caused
by Canada's climate have been mentioned. Find out
how much snow-removal from the streets costs per
year in the city nearest you. Suggest ways by which
technology might develop a method of overcoming
this continuing source of expense in Canada.*

ploughs to keep the tracks clear and as a result the snow was piled high
on each side of the track. This accumulation of snow prevented
carriages and wagons from using the street. The storekeepers were
naturally unhappy because they lost business to their competitors
whose establishments were not located along the line of the street
railway.

During a particularly heavy snowfall in February 1881 the shopkeepers became more than usually irritated with the situation. After
an unscheduled and informal meeting of the Yonge Street merchants
a plan of action was adopted. All along Yonge Street store employees
came out into the thoroughfare waving their shovels and shouting at
the horse-car drivers. Then they began to shovel all the snow that had
piled up on the roadway back onto the tracks. In addition, the shopkeepers pushed many of the cars off the track and filled them with snow.

Infuriated by the actions of the storekeepers, the horse-car drivers jumped out of their vehicles and began to fight. In the battle that resulted the drivers were doomed to defeat simply because they were so easily outnumbered. Although some pent-up anger was undoubtedly released, the actions of the merchants did little to solve the problem.

In addition to the problem of snow removal, the horse-drawn car had some serious drawbacks. In the first place, service tended to be slow. In theory the cars were supposed to run at intervals of forty minutes. In practice the service was not geared to a timetable of any sort. For many passengers this flexibility was a decided advantage and indeed one of the attractions of this particular form of transportation. For those who depended on the horse cars to get them to work on time and to hurry them home for dinner at the end of the day, the slow service was at the very least frustrating—it was neither reliable nor rapid enough.

This was not the only problem connected with the operation of the street railway. Perhaps the most serious shortcoming was the limited area serviced by the horse cars. Most urban centres had only a few miles of track on the busiest streets. Until the area covered by the street railway was expanded, people were still confined to the city centre.

In the meantime the bicycle craze was changing the habits and life style of many Canadians. 'Health and strength were in every revolution of its pedal,' wrote J. S. Brierly, the first Honourable Secretary of the Canadian Wheelmen's Association, 'and appetite grew with the miles we covered. There was an exhilaration in the new method of locomotion that made all devotees of the sport.' Such was the enthusiasm for the bicycle that 'everywhere clubs were advocated and farmers' horses were slowly educated in the knowledge that it was not necessary to jump into the adjoining field to escape the shining apparition.'

In Montreal the first cycling club, Winged Wheel Knights, was established in the late 1870s. The seriousness with which the bicycle was regarded is captured in a poem written by Arthur Weir for the Montreal Club:

> On steeds of steel, in country ways,
> Far from the City's street
> The Winged Wheel Knights, on summer days,
> The awestruck peasants meet;

Montreal bicycle club, 1885.
*What do you notice about the way the men are
dressed? Why did they dress in this way?*

> *And hills in vain their bulk upraise*
> *To tire the rapid feet*
> *That o'er the dusty roadways chase*
> *The birds, well nigh as fleet.*

By the turn of the century Toronto cyclists were enjoying weekend excursions to outlying districts, thanks to the development of 'Safety Bicycles' with pneumatic rubber tires. These new tires were reasonably durable and even if a flat should occur, it was fairly easy to make repairs on the spot. After a carefree picnic along a country road the refreshed cyclists were ready for the return to the city. A new sense of freedom and mobility had been given to city residents and the countryside was now within reasonable reach of the energetic cyclist.

Aside from the sheer pleasure of it, many other uses were found for this new form of transportation. Around the turn of the century the telephone was being used increasingly; the number of people with telephones in Montreal, for example, had increased from 3,000 in 1890 to over 30,000 by 1910. The busy housewife could now purchase most of her needs by telephone and arrange to have them delivered to the house. Small storekeepers began to hire young men with bicycles to deliver packages throughout the city, although the large stores, like Eaton's, still used horse-drawn vehicles to make deliveries.

The police force in many cities also found the bicycle advantageous for patrolling city streets and answering complaints far from head-quarters. The taxpayers were happy about this change for two reasons. First, bicycles were much cheaper to purchase and operate than horses, who had to be fed and housed. Secondly the bicycle did not have to be saddled and some reasoned that this would lead to faster service.

For many ordinary city residents the bicycle facilitated the move from the core of the urban centre to the suburbs. In 1899 the Winnipeg *Free Press* argued that 'No more remarkable development has been witnessed in our city than the growth in the use of the bicycle. It has furnished a new means of locomotion, has solved for many people the problem of rapid transit in the city.' It is interesting that in recent years the bicycle has enjoyed a 'comeback' among city residents.

As late as the 1880s Montreal preserved the basic outline of the city as it had been found two hundred years before. Its interests, however, had changed. Over the years fur had given way to wheat as the basis of trade and the canoe had vanished in the wake of the steamship. Within the boundaries of the city lived a comfortable community engaged primarily in trade and commerce. But this unhurried and prosperous existence was slowly and steadily changing as manufacturing came to occupy an important place in the financial life of the city.

With the rapid growth of textile mills, furniture factories, rolling mills and the CPR shops came the urgent demand of businessmen for more and more workers. This call was enthusiastically answered by hundreds of young men who were eager to leave family farms that could no longer adequately support them. Despite the warnings of parents and parish priests about the godlessness of city life, many young

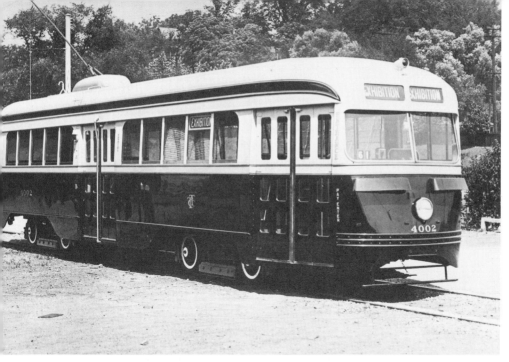

A modern streetcar, Toronto.
Name other cities that have vehicles running on tracks in the road. Which cities have replaced such vehicles? Why have they done this?

French-Canadian men felt no great attachment to the land and were reluctant to face a future that offered only a meagre existence. These were the men who annually made their way to Montreal in increasing numbers in the hope of a steady cash income and a more comfortable life.

The same thing happened in many Canadian cities. The farmer was turning into a factory worker and in the already crowded urban centres he found both work and lodgings; few ever returned to rural life. This serious problem of overcrowding in many cities was further aggravated by the rapid increase in the number of immigrants. In one year alone more than 96,000 immigrants arrived, and most of them settled in Montreal, Toronto, or Winnipeg. Often the accommodation to house this great influx of people into the urban centres was pitifully inadequate: the pressure of a growing population first showed up in the inadequacy of housing facilities.

In the latter part of the nineteenth century and into the twentieth century the business district grew in both importance and size in every city. There were few advocates of town planning in those days and as a consequence cities grew without direction or thought for the future. Streets remained narrow, parks were few in number, and the shores of lakes and rivers were spoiled forever by factories and railway lines. Industries of every size and description were attracted by the facilities of the 'downtown' area, and in their wake they brought noise, dirt, traffic, and further overcrowding.

With the invasion of industry into the city, there was a growing desire on the part of city residents to leave the now smoke-filled and polluted centre for new residential areas around the city fringe. At first only the rich could afford the cost of commuting, and they were the first to move to the suburbs. The poor stayed in the city and walked. And so the segregation of residential districts by class or wealth began. But even the rich would have found commuting difficult if it had not been for the next great improvement in city transportation.

Around the turn of the century the old horse-drawn street cars that had once been so popular were giving way to a new form of transport— the electric railway. The public reponse to this change was again warmly enthusiastic. The new cars were much wider than the horse cars 'and a man of ordinary dimensions,' reported the *Globe*, 'can sit reasonably cross legged in them without his boot in the shin of his travelling companion on the opposite side.' Many passengers greatly appreciated the springs and generous padding in the cushions, while others remarked favourably on the leather straps that hung from the roof for the safety and comfort of standing passengers.

Although the advantages of the electric railway were obvious, some feared that the number of accidents would increase because of the speed of the new vehicles. And in fact on the first day of operation of the electric railway in Toronto a man was seriously injured when he leaned too far into the path of the approaching vehicle to get a closer look at the new contraption. Not everyone was willing to admit that the days of the horse as a means of transportation were drawing to an end. Those who loved horses were reluctant to see them replaced, and those who were in the business of selling the animals to the street-railway companies feared the loss of their livelihood. 'What will be the result

A modern subway train, Toronto.
What are the advantages and disadvantages of this form of transportation?

of the trolley's application to King, Queen, and Yonge Streets?' asked one of Toronto's newspapers. 'The trolley will drive carriages off these streets, decrease the value of property, and increase the danger to life. . . . It is a mistake to accept it, and it will be a curse when it does come.' Despite these gloomy predictions the electric railway became a part of city transportation and by 1894 the last horse-drawn cars disappeared from Toronto streets.

Despite the improvements in transportation that facilitated the move from the downtown core to the outlying districts, many cities were facing the grave problems that accompanied their rapid growth in population. Urban poverty and the related problems of high unemployment and inadequate housing were now very serious.

In 1915 a report on housing conditions in Montreal indicated that 'Housing conditions have degenerated and there is a decided lack of workingmen's dwellings with proper conveniences at low rental. Rents have increased by fifty per cent in the last seven years, leading to a doubling up of families in the same apartment or house, causing overcrowding and ill health.' The story was much the same in other urban centres across the country, and how could it be otherwise? In 1901 there were only fifty-eight cities in Canada with a population of

Ford Model T, 1925.
Explain how cars have been improved since 1925.

over 5,000; in 1911 there were ninety. In 1911 Montreal had almost half a million residents. Toronto had doubled in size between 1901 and 1911; Winnipeg was four times larger than it had been in 1901 and Vancouver had expanded only slightly less in the same ten-year period. The newer cities on the Prairies, like Calgary and Regina, increased ten times in the decade between 1901 and 1911.

There were those who saw the dangers inherent in this type of rapid growth. 'Many will tell you that we in Toronto are free from slums,' argued one early reformer, 'but they are only shutting their eyes to evils that exist. Some of these vile hovels are old cottages built 60 years ago and not improved in any way since—floors sunk, walls out of shape, plaster off, windows broken.' In such squalor the urban poor fell easy prey to diseases of all kinds.

The tragedy of the urban poor, then as now, was that *the majority of them are honest and willing to work. . . . It is not to be presumed that all who desire employment can procure it in Toronto;*

the contrary being really the case because labour and skill of almost any kind are here in excess. For every position of regular labour there are at least five applicants.

Despite a recognition of the problem on the part of some Canadians, little of a concrete nature was done to ease the situation. Aside from charitable and church-affiliated organizations there was no assistance for the poor. Welfare and unemployment insurance were either pitifully inadequate or completely non-existent at this time.

In contrast to Toronto and Montreal, with their swelling population and growing social problems, Halifax was changing at a slower and more reasonable pace.

The streets were still unpaved except in the tram car tracks, muddy in spring and autumn, swirling with dust in the summer winds. The business section and some of the residential streets had flagstone or concrete sidewalks ... but everywhere else the townsfolk strolled on paths of household cinders, dumped by the city's collection wagons and casually raked level. The automobile had made its appearance, but it was still a minor factor in the traffic. There were no motor-trucks at all. The city fire-fighting equipment was still horse-drawn and the alarm was sounded over the city by bells in the fire hall towers, ringing the exact location by a code that every resident kept handy for reference. Five years later motor cars were everywhere in Halifax and 'the mixture of horse and motor traffic in the downtown area brought the traffic policeman into existence. . . .'

The motor car was also becoming a common sight on city streets elsewhere in Canada, despite the shrill opposition of horse lovers. 'Replace the horse!' they cried. 'Have you ever heard of anything so ridiculous in your life?' Others branded the automobile as 'the device of the devil'. And many were the voices declaring that you will 'never get me into one of those contraptions! Dang fool thing's liable to blow up. . . !'

The automobile, however, was an exciting and important innovation because of its speed and comfort, but especially because of the freedom it offered. It was no less exciting because of the numerous breakdowns and punctured tires that invariably accompanied a short jaunt to the countryside. And men like Adolphus Burgoyne of Belleville were proud to be the first in their community to own a 'tin lizzie'. As he and others like him drove down the streets of their home town they were oblivious to the 'cloud of white smoke and evil smelling fumes' that followed in their wake.

The roads were at first the worst enemy of the automobile. There were few miles of pavement. Roads were narrow and winding and the spring and autumn mud still caused serious problems for travellers. More than one pleasant Sunday drive was spoiled when the Model T became firmly stuck in the glutinous mud. As in the days of the old stage coach, everyone climbed out of the vehicle and set to work to free the car by using nearby fence rails as levers. In spite of such obvious drawbacks, the compulsion to buy an automobile affected all who could afford the luxury and many who could not. For just under four hundred dollars a man could buy a 'flivver' of his own. From the very beginning the motor car was a status symbol that few could resist. But when some of these first cars came noisily chugging out of the city at the furious speed of twelve miles an hour, they created clouds of dust and terrified the horses as they passed buggies and wagons. Not surprisingly the local farmers were inclined to regard them as an unwelcome nuisance.

The motor car brought other changes into Canadian life as well. Criminal activity took on an entirely new dimension with the aid of the automobile. Vancouver police reported in 1919 at least six robberies a night in which the culprits made their 'getaway' in a car. To keep up with the criminal element in society, police forces across the country soon purchased automobiles. And old horse-drawn fire vehicles slowly gave way to the fire truck. This improvement no doubt saved much property and loss of life by speeding up the arrival of firefighters at the scene of a fire. One not-so-pleasant result of automobiles was that the seeds of many weeds and noxious plants were inadvertently carried from one area to another in the treads of the tires. And the motor car also brought problems that would appear more serious in the future— traffic congestion and pollution.

In 1903 there were only 220 motor vehicles registered in Canada; by 1920 there were more than 400,000. With the automobile came the ever-increasing demand for paved roads and the desire of the city

Downtown Winnipeg traffic congestion.
*Farmers found the early cars a menace. In what ways
are cars a menace today?*

dweller for 'a place in the country'. Many municipalities sprinkled
unpaved roads with oil to keep the dust down to a minimum until
roads could be improved. As roads were improved, the automobile
became another factor in stimulating suburban living because of the
enormous mobility it provided.

To help visualize urban growth one should think in terms of
populations expanding outward from the downtown core, although
this development was often uneven—more rapid growth might occur,
perhaps, in the areas east or north of the city. The first areas of growth,
the suburbs that the rich first moved into—districts like Yorkville and
Rosedale in Toronto, and Westmount in Montreal—became incor-
porated into the cities as new, more outlying suburbs developed,
although the first suburbs still kept their character as prestige residential areas. Without the improvements in transportation—the electric
railway and later the car—the size of Canadian cities would have been
limited. And with this movement from the city centre, town and
country were brought into a new and more immediate relationship.

Steam-operated fire engine, 1871.
What advances have been made in today's fire-fighting equipment?

The third major wave of suburban development took place more than twenty-five years after the two just described. Scores of thousands of immigrants made their way to Canada after the Second World War and changed the nature of urban life. To accommodate all these people the cities expanded at an unbelievable rate. Reasonably priced homes had to be constructed as rapidly as possibly. Building lots in the cities were both few in number and high in cost. Again, people looked to the undeveloped land that lay beyond the city itself.

Since the Second World War more than two million immigrants have come to Canada from other lands. They came by ship and by airplane from the four corners of the globe. While the largest single group of these 'new Canadians' has come from the United Kingdom, great numbers of Italians, Germans, Dutch, and Poles have also taken up residence in Canada. Unlike earlier immigrants who settled in the Prairies, these post-war immigrants did not come with the goal of developing prosperous farms. Rather they came with the expressed intention of living and working in an urban industrial environment, so they settled in urban centres.

Given these facts it is not surprising that Montreal and Toronto, Canada's two largest cities, have become the homes of great numbers of these immigrants. In 1961, for example, 42 per cent of the residents of Toronto were not born in Canada. That this immigration to urban centres has had consequences for the nature of the city is easily demonstrated.

To begin with, immigration in the post-war era has been partly responsible for the prosperity evident in our cities. New immigrants need houses, clothes, and food. As a consequence more people must be employed to meet these needs. To a certain extent this explains the new buildings and suburbs that can be seen in parts of Canada.

In addition to providing a general stimulus to Canadian economic development, immigration has benefited Canada in others ways. Quite often certain skills required for economic development were in short supply in Canadian cities and the skilled craftsmen who came from the factories of England, Scotland, or Germany were invaluable to industrial development. Canada has also profited from the knowledge of scientists and engineers who grew up and were trained in foreign lands.

Perhaps less obvious than the economic consequences of immigration are the cultural effects. At first one might even doubt that Canadian culture has in any way been affected by immigration. Yet one only has to appreciate that the 'pizzeria', for example, has become commonplace in most urban centres to see this claim partially refuted. Moreover, in larger cities it is not uncommon to encounter dozens of restaurants serving the food of different nations. Before the war a restaurant serving Italian, Hungarian, or Greek cuisine was difficult to locate even in a number of our largest cities.

Because immigrants were not, upon arrival in Canada, usually very well off financially, they were compelled to find housing wherever it was least expensive. In Toronto and some other cities there was an influx of immigrants into the downtown area where accommodation was cheap. Later large numbers of immigrants were able to join the more general exodus from the downtown core into the suburbs.

A group of firemen outside an early fire-hall.
Who is responsible for operating fire services today?
What factors make fires less likely in homes today
than in the nineteenth century? What factors make
fires more likely?

It is possible to argue that a rapid expansion of suburbs did more to change the nature of post-war Canadian cities than did immigration. In urban centres all across the country people were making an effort to get out of the downtown areas and into the suburbs. What was left in the city core were pockets of low-income housing, pockets of high-class residential districts, and industrial and financial centres thronged with people by day and almost totally deserted at night. In Toronto, for example, the residential population of the downtown part of the city, despite immigration, actually decreased between 1945 and the early 1960s, while the population of the suburbs outside of the downtown area rose considerably. This movement to the suburbs was assisted to a large degree by the rapid expansion of public transportation in the form of extended bus lines. In Toronto alone suburban service has increased 'by an average of a million miles each year since 1945, a rate unmatched anywhere in North America'. In 1968 the Toronto Transit Commission estimated that more than seventy-eight million people had travelled on the suburban bus routes alone. In Toronto, at least, suburban development has gone hand in hand with improved transportation networks.

The reasons people had for making this move to the suburbs were many and varied. There is no doubt that some were lured from the city by the promise of a better life for themselves and their children. This is clearly reflected in the statement of one Toronto suburbanite to a researcher. 'Bought a house,' he explained, 'to give the child a home and be my own master. Had an apartment at Bloor and Spadina. It wasn't what we were used to; lived there to save money to get the house as fast as possible.' Sentiments similar to these were expressed by another suburban dweller who hoped that the change of environment would result in an improvement in the quality of family life. 'The house we were renting was pleasant,' but 'we wanted a better atmosphere in which to raise our son. The house was on a busy through street. We didn't know many people in the area.' To city-dwellers such as these, movement to the suburbs was made possible because of improvements in transportation. Even if they worked downtown, wide, easily travelled roads and expressways, buses and, in the case of Toronto and Montreal, a subway, have made it possible to live some distance from the place of work.

To other suburban residents, the decision to move was prompted more by economic considerations than by concern with the quality of the neighbourhood. 'We bought this house,' one resident admitted, 'because it was all we could afford. We liked the house—the floor plan and brick outside. We knew absolutely nothing about the area. Got information from fellows my husband worked with. This place we got out of the paper.' Likewise a resident of the same area commented that 'We chose this house because it was cheap.' For some, then, the move to the suburbs was prompted by a desire to live in a better neighbourhood. For others the price of housing was foremost in deciding where they would move.

Whatever the reason for the initial move, it is not surprising that people accepted suburban life with varying degrees of enthusiasm. One woman was fairly optimistic about her new neighbourhood. 'I like this district,' she stated. 'We ain't got no problems here. When we came from Cosburn Avenue it was a rough place, no water no nothing. Take a look at it now.' By way of contrast, another woman was discontented with her new surroundings and complained that she preferred city life. The reason for her preference was simple. 'Here one is too tied down with children,' she explained. 'It is so far to drag them to the plaza. In the city I never minded taking them shopping. It is very hard to keep in touch with friends or relations,' she continued. 'I really miss my mother and sister. We could visit back and forth in the city but we can't here. Also my mother could mind the children and let me have a day off. This cannot happen here. People will not phone long distance to say they are coming out and when they do come they stay too long.' For this woman the advantages that might be offered by suburban living were clearly outweighed by disadvantages. Unlike her husband, who probably commuted by car to his job, she was 'stuck' with relatively little to absorb her time and talents.

But it should not be assumed that this experience was typical. In another suburban community a woman gave quite a different account of her life.

I didn't know a soul when I came here. I got to know the woman two doors down the street I guess because she has a child of the same age and we're the same age. And then I joined the Ladies' Auxiliary and got to know some more people. I see some of the neighbours once or twice a day. There is a lot of visiting. Some of the women are never home. I got to know some more people through going to the Post Office. There are showers, I get invited to all of them.

Although large numbers of Canadians currently live in suburbs such as the ones described here, it should not be assumed that the majority do so. Great numbers still live in other areas of the city, in small towns and villages, and on farms. But since the end of the Second World War the development of the suburb has, perhaps, been one of the most easily recognized changes in the Canadian scene. As has been the case in other countries, this development has been greatly facilitated by the increasing use of the automobile and by the improvement of roads, highways, and expressways. Improvements in public transportation—buses and in some cities the subway—have done much to assist the flow of traffic between the home and the place of work.

9 Harvesters and Trucks

Life was also changing outside the urban centres. Before the turn of the century the demands of rural life required little beyond the basic understanding of reading, writing, and arithmetic. The young men quit school, many before completing grade eight, and began working on the family farm. In those days a well-equipped farm boasted a spade, an axe, hoes, and a 'heavy barrow [plough] made of three timbers fastened in the form of a triangle and fitted with iron teeth and drawn by oxen'.

The nature of farming has changed in Canada since 1900 because of changes in agricultural technology. Today tractors and combines (reapers and threshers) quickly do the work that was formerly done slowly by men and horses. The transition to 'modern' farming was a long and painstaking process. At first many farmers were reluctant to make the necessary capital investment in machinery, although the first tractors could plough five times as much per day as a dependable team of horses. But farmers slowly came to the realization that the horse, like the ox, had had his day. The cost of a horse's feed, harness, stable, and medical bills had all increased over the years. As one farmer put it, 'Nothing that concerns the horse has remained the same except his power. He is not one pound stronger than he was thirty years ago, in the days of his cheapness.'

A very early threshing machine.
Although the use of these machines was more efficient than threshing by hand, why was the size of wheat farms still limited when this was the only kind of equipment available?

In the Prairies the move to mechanization was prompted in part by the lack of available horses. In 1913 a farmer wrote:

In Western Canada we find the shortage of horses most conspicuous. To plow the 200,000,000 new acres ... requires the power of 4,000,000 horses—twice as many horses as there are in the whole Dominion of Canada. There is absolutely no way for this new vast region to develop itself, except by the use of tractors.

A steam-threshing outfit, 1898.
How many men were required to get in the harvest?

As farming became more and more mechanized, farming operations on a large scale became more profitable than small farms. Today, farmers are beginning to regard agriculture as a sophisticated business enterprise based on an understanding of scientific principles. The modern farmer has to be an agricultural specialist, and he requires formal training in agricultural technology and sound business methods. He must be educated in order to make important decisions about new 'improved' seeds and the most suitable variety of fertilizer for particular crops planted in specific types of soil under certain weather conditions. Today's farmer has been fortunate in that several universities, like the one in Guelph, Ontario, have carried on extensive scientific research to assist the farmer in controlling weeds and insects and in generally improving his final product, whether it be chickens or soy beans. Agricultural experts are presently working hand in hand with the farmers of southwestern Ontario to test the feasibility of peanut

145

A modern combine-harvester.
In what ways have these machines contributed to
rural depopulation over the past fifty years?

production in the area. Much of this research has been made possible with the generous financial support of the government.

The increasing use of labour-saving machinery in agriculture has been responsible, in part, for the depopulation of rural areas. Four years after the combine harvester was introduced into the Prairies, for example, fifty thousand farm labourers lost their jobs. In addition the growth of large-scale farming operations has made it increasingly difficult for the small family farm to survive as a competitive entity. 'It is the machinery, combined with the scientific methods and large units of production, from which farm profits are being derived,' explained one farmer. 'Small farmers, with small and old-fashioned operations, are making no profits at all.' And as we have seen, the city

146

seemed to offer greater economic opportunities than the restricted life of the family farm; people from less profitable farms joined the unemployed farm labourers in the exodus from the countryside.

One rural resident described how changes in technology and the move to the cities changed life in the villages in the 1930s:

The mechanization of agriculture had done away with village industries and reduced the number of men required on the farm. A few decades ago our country villages had their carriage shops, their tanneries, their harness shops, and a number of other small industries employing from one to perhaps five people. Besides the village industries, there was a considerable amount of home production on the farm which occupied the time of the farmer and his family between seasons. For example, the men used to make lumber and shingles and the women used to spin. Such occupations provided work in slack seasons, gave variety to country life, and increased the farmer's income. All this has changed: many of the village shops and a number of the small industries have closed down. The once prosperous village store-keeper, whose place of business served as a social centre, has been forced into bankruptcy because of the popularity of the catalogue mail-order system. As one rural observer remarked, 'cheap and rapid transit made the mail order system possible. The one-price system and exact description in advertising, together with a large turnover and direct service, made it efficient.'

Changes in rural life, however, did not end here. One of the most difficult problems that had been faced by early farmers in Canada, wherever they had settled, was loneliness. Social contact with neighbours was limited and farmers made only infrequent trips to a nearby town, and then only to conduct simple business transactions. By 1920 the social isolation of the farmer was beginning to break down through the introduction of mail deliveries, telephones, radios, and automobiles to the countryside. The telephone did much to provide rural residents with some of the conveniences of urban life. The doctor, the dentist, and the department store were now as close to the farmer and his family as the nearest telephone. The radio made possible a far wider range of entertainment than the 'backwoods' farmer could ever have dreamed of, and it was pointed out that 'the fact that one can

147

Abandoned nineteenth-century farm near Toronto.
*Why would it no longer be profitable to operate
this farm?*

tune in almost any city in the continent does a great deal to break down the sense of social isolation so often experienced in the country.'

In earlier times a carriage pulled by a horse usually travelled about four miles an hour over dusty or muddy roads, depending upon the weather conditions. With the use of the car and with the improvement in country roads all this changed. How great a change this was is shown by the remarks of one progressive-minded farmer, who wrote in 1930:

People who regard automobiles and radios as gross extravagances should remember the way these things are helping to enlarge the small community. We have stopped measuring distances in miles and are measuring them in minutes and hours.

There were many farmers who were skeptical of these so-called improvements. After all, they argued, they had managed quite well before. But most rural residents were quite conscious of the importance

Abandoned railway tracks.
Apart from competition from trucking companies, what other difficulties are railroads facing today?

of good roads in their community even if they did not own a car. One farmer urged:

There should be good roads. This not only makes the community accessible to other folk, but people frequently gather impressions of it simply by driving through, and the roads are the first thing that impresses them. Good roads are not only a great convenience to the residents themselves but they become an object of community pride and a source of satisfaction and rural contentment.

Good roads had economic as well as social effects. The farmer of today is able to transport his produce via large, refrigerated transport trucks along super-highways to markets hundreds or even thousands of miles away. (One side effect is that people in the cities are able to obtain fresh meat, milk, fruit, and vegetables daily.) But this development in turn affected other means of transportation. The railways, once

A rural railway station in Ontario that has been closed down.
*Some railway stations are also being closed now in
the centres of big cities.
Why was the railway station in the centre of Ottawa
closed? What is the building used for now?*

the transportation backbone of Canada, found themselves facing stiff competition from the trucking companies. To eliminate unnecessary costs, the railways adopted a policy of abandoning branch lines that were no longer economically viable. Just as the coming of the railway had stimulated settlements, so the closing of lines eliminated the reason for the existence of some villages, and most of their residents joined the migration to the urban centres.

Two basic institutions of rural life, the church and the one-room school house, also underwent serious changes. The mobility that car ownership provided for country people meant that they no longer had to confine their social activities to their closest community. Some rural

A nineteenth-century one-room schoolhouse.
This building has now been converted to a country home.
Why was this done rather than tearing it down?

people, for example, preferred to worship in the larger churches of a nearby town or city. Those who wished to continue to attend their small country church found that they could no longer afford the expenses involved. As the congregation became smaller and smaller, there were not enough people left to support the salary of a minister and to find the money to pay for the upkeep of the building. As the years passed it became increasingly difficult to find a qualified minister who would accept a country congregation. In the face of such difficulties many rural churches have been compelled to close their doors, and many community activities that were based on the church have ceased.

Similarly the one-room school house has virtually disappeared in many parts of rural Canada. The migration of rural people to the cities, combined with the general decrease in the size of families, has meant that there are not enough children in one area to justify keeping a school open. It became difficult, moreover, to attract qualified teachers to small country schools: firstly because they were, as a rule, paid less than their urban counterparts; secondly because there were not as many opportunities for promotion in the country; and thirdly because urban living was more attractive to many people. Yet it was becoming important that children brought up in the country should have as good an education as those brought up in the city, both for those who would become farmers, as we have seen, and for those who would eventually go to live in the city.

Large centrally located schools, equipped with the most up-to-date teaching aids and offering a wide range of subject matter, have found their way to the countryside. The opening of these new centres of education would not have been possible without the means to transport children from a wide area—the school bus is a familiar sight on concession roads. Most rural residents are pleased with this change and many feel that their children are receiving a better education than was formerly available to them.

However, the disappearance of the family farm and the closing of the one-room schools and the churches has had other effects on rural life. The sense of community that was at one time reinforced by both the church and the school is gradually disintegrating. Christmas pageants, church picnics, and bazaars are, in many areas, no longer events of community significance. Some feel that these changes are not beneficial and mark the end of an era—an era in which the farmer had an important status in society that he is now losing. Others, however, argue that changes in rural life have been beneficial. As one farmer put it, 'we don't farm the same, travel the same, or find our social life in the same places.' These people feel that changes in Canadian society in general have brought greater prosperity and a higher standard of living for all Canadians.

How can one assess the satisfaction of the farmer who once walked across his fertile fields secure in the knowledge that his son and his son after him would continue the operation of the farm? Equally, how can one assess the improvements in the social life of Canadians, both rural and urban, that developments in technology have made possible? There is no one answer. Each individual must decide for himself or herself what has been lost and what has been gained from the time the white man first landed in Canada to the highly mobile, technologically advanced, and pollution-ridden society of today.

152

For Discussion, Study, or Research

I

CANOES AND SNOWSHOES

1.

So God created man in His own image, in the image of God created He him; male and female created He them.

And God blessed them, and God said unto them, Be fruitful, and multiply, and replenish the earth, and subdue it: and have dominion over the fish of the sea, and over the fowl of the air, and over every living thing that moveth upon the earth.

And God said, Behold, I have given you every herb bearing seed, which is upon the face of all the earth, and every tree, in the which is the fruit of a tree yielding seed; to you it shall be for meat.

GENESIS 1:27-29

What attitude to nature is shown by this quotation from the Bible? Try to find quotations from other works that show the white man's attitudes to nature. Compare these attitudes with those of the Indians shown in the legends in this chapter and in any others you can find. Were the attitudes of all the Indian tribes the same?

How might our attitude to nature affect the way we regard pollution and other ecological problems today? Would the Indians have had the same kinds of problems if they had been left in possession of Canada? Why?

2. In what ways did the fur trade, new forms of transportation, and European tools and customs change the Indian way of life?

Extract from *Robinson Treaty Made in the Year 1850 with the Ojibewa Indians of Lake Superior Conveying Certain Lands to the Crown*, p. 3, Queen's Printer, IAND Pub. No. Q5-0581-000-EE-A.

That for and in consideration of the sum of two thousand pounds of good and lawful money of Upper Canada, to them in hand paid, and for the further perpetual annuity of five hundred pounds, the same to be paid and delivered to the said Chiefs and their Tribes at a convenient season of each summer, not later than the first day of August at the Honorable the Hudson's Bay Company's Posts of Michipicoton and Fort William, they the said chiefs and principal men do freely, fully and voluntarily surrender, cede, grant and convey unto Her Majesty, Her heirs and successors forever, all their right, title and interest in the whole of the territory above described, save and except the reservations set forth in the schedule hereunto annexed, which reservations shall be held and occupied by the said Chiefs and their Tribes in common, for the purpose of residence and cultivation,—and should the said Chiefs and their respective Tribes at any time desire to dispose of any mineral or other valuable productions upon the said reservations, the same will be at their request sold by order of the Superintendent General of the Indian Department for the time being, for their sole use and benefit, and to the best advantage.

And the said William Benjamin Robinson of the first part, on behalf of Her Majesty and the Government of this Province, hereby promises and agrees to make the payments as before mentioned; and further to allow the said chiefs and their tribes the full and free privilege to hunt over the territory now ceded by them, and to fish in the waters thereof as they have heretofore been in the habit of doing, saving and excepting only such portions of the said territory as may from time to time be sold or leased to individuals, or companies of individuals, and occupied by them with the consent of the Provincial Government. The parties of the second part further promise and agree that they will not sell, lease, or otherwise dispose of any portion of their reservations without the consent of the Superintendent General of Indian Affairs being first had and obtained; nor will they at any time hinder or prevent persons from exploring or searching for mineral or other valuable productions in any part of the territory hereby ceded to Her Majesty as before mentioned. The parties of the second part also agree that in case the Government of this Province should before the date of this agreement have sold, or bargained to sell, any mining locations or other property on the portions of the territory hereby reserved for their use

154

and benefit, then and in that case such sale, or promise of sale, shall be forfeited, if the parties interested desire it, by the Government, and the amount accruing therefrom shall be paid to the tribe to whom the reservation belongs.

Why were treaties made with the Indians? Since the Indian had no real concept of land ownership, do you think the Indians were treated fairly by the government in 1850? Examine some of the other treaties made with other Indian tribes. To what extent are treaties to blame for Indian problems today? What claims are Indians making today on the federal government because of these treaties?

Is it possible for the Indians to preserve their own way of life? What effect has living on reservations had on the Indian way of life? Why have Indians formed movements like 'Red Power' and what do they hope to gain by them?

3. Contrast the way of life of the west-coast tribes with that of tribes on the Prairies and that of the eastern Indian tribes. What features of the landscape, and the different forms of animal and vegetable life would account for these differences? How did the transportation needs of the Indian tribes differ because of their environment?

Chapter 1 tells how a birch-bark canoe was built. These methods are sometimes still used, almost unchanged, today. For an account of how a modern birch-bark canoe is built today, see *The Beaver*, Summer 1973, pp. 50-3. Find out what other kinds of canoes are available today (size, construction materials). What special needs are these canoes designed for? Where are they used?

In 1967, to celebrate the first 100 years of Confederation, a centenary journey across the whole of Canada was undertaken by groups of young Canadians. Wherever possible canoes were used, ranging from the standard sixteen-foot size to twenty-six-foot voyageur models for the Lake Superior section. A beaver pelt was passed from group to group as each completed its section of the trip. The pelt travelled from the Maritimes to Victoria. Some of the sections completed by canoe are listed below, together with accounts of two of the trips. A log of the entire Centenary Journey can be obtained from The Canadian Camping Association, Suite 203, 102 Eglinton Avenue East, Toronto

12, Ontario. On a topographical map, plot the course of a section of the trip in your province. How could you have told from the map, in advance of the journey, that portages would be necessary? What modern hazards were encountered that earlier travellers by canoe would not have met? Compare these accounts with those of some of the explorers who travelled by canoe.

PRINCE EDWARD ISLAND	Savage Harbour to Banshaw
NOVA SCOTIA	Dartmouth to Shubenacadie
	Shubenacadie to Maitland
	Parrsboro to River Hebert
NEW BRUNSWICK	Saint John River to Fort Beausejour
	Fort Kent, Maine to Saint John, New Brunswick
QUEBEC	Notre Dame du Portage, Quebec to Edmunston, N.B.
	Britannia Bay to Montreal
	Deux Rivières to Deep River
ONTARIO	Mattawa to Lac Talon
	North Bay to Georgian Bay
	Sault Ste Marie to Wawa
	Lac La Croix to Fort Frances
MANITOBA	Grand Rapids to Le Pas
	Winnipeg River to Lake Winnipeg
SASKATCHEWAN	Pelican Narrows, Sask., to Le Pas, Manitoba
	Otter Rapids to Pelican Narrows Townsite
	Pinehouse Lake to Otter Rapids
ALBERTA	Vega Ferry to Athabaska
	Whitecourt to Vega Ferry
	Hinton to Whitecourt
BRITISH COLUMBIA	Alberta Border to Quesnel on the Fraser River
	Squamish to Williamson's Landing
	Goldstream Park to Victoria

LAC LA CROIX TO FORT FRANCES
Leaving from Painted Rock campsite it is possible to avoid open water and to save some distance by passing south of Coleman Island following the left hand shore around to the narrower part of the large. The narrow portion of Lac la Croix is full of hundreds of islands, many of which have good campsites. The paddle from Painted

Rock campsite to Beatty Portage (fifty yards, marine railway) is about twenty-five miles and takes six to seven hours with reasonable winds. This time could be considerably increased by bad winds.

A paddle of six miles through Loon Lake leads to Loon Falls, a portage of seventy-five rods, and the Loon River. The Loon River is an interesting paddle of about fifteen miles taking four hours or so. (It is possible to follow the old Dawson Trail portage, now a truck road—six miles, from Wilkins Bay of Lac la Croix to Portage Bay of Sand Point Lake, saving some fifteen miles of travel.) There is a Canada Customs base on the north shore of Portage Bay.

At Harrison Narrows we again have a choice of route—go straight north on Sand Point Lake to Namakan Narrows and into Namakan Lake or, strike out northwest into Grassy Bay and take the short portage from its end into Namakan Lake.

With reasonable winds the paddle from Namakan Narrows through the twelve mile length of Namakan Lake to Squaw Narrows takes about three hours. A further two hours paddle takes us through Squirrel Narrows and Kettle Channel to Rainy Lake.

In paddling the roughly forty miles on Rainy Lake to Fort Frances it is advisable to stay as close as possible to the U.S. shore as storms can come up rather quickly and Rainy Lake is very big and open.

Canada's Centenary Journey, Canadian Camping Association, 1971, p. 85.

OTTER RAPIDS TO PELICAN NARROWS TOWNSITE

We travelled by road to Missinipi just below Otter Rapids, and paddled with fine weather to the portage at Robertson Falls. After crossing the portage, we passaged a fishing camp just beyond, and later stopped at the Cree village of Stanley. Here we visited the imposing Anglican Church and the Hudson's Bay Company and Co-op stores. Several Indian rock paintings are still visible above Stanley Rapids. We used rollers to drag our canoes around the rapids, and paddled into Drope Lake, on the south shore of which is an abandoned Uranium mine.

We lunched at the mouth of the Rapid River, where we photographed the picturesque Nistowiak Falls. Supplies are available at the Drinking Falls Churchill River Lodge at the outlet of Nistowiak Lake.

The end of the third day saw us over the Grand Portage and into Trade Lake, where the historic Frog Portage led us to the narrow, sluggish beginnings of the Sturgeon-Weir system. Below Wood Lake, where the channel is broken by a series of three short rapids, we caught several pickerel.

A few miles above Pelican Narrows, we shot the exciting Medicine Rapids, and shortly afterwards landed at the townsite of Pelican Narrows, which may now be reached by road and a bridge over the narrows.

Ibid., p. 102.

II

SLEIGHS AND RAFTS

1.   Describe the kind of people who came from France. How were they chosen? What did they come to New France to do? Compare the climate of Quebec with that of France. How did the settlers adapt to Canada's climate? Why were the settlers prepared to endure the hardships of New France?

The settlers brought with them one important invention that the Indians did not have—the wheel. How would the use of the wheel explain the differences between the way of life of the French and the Indians? What other factors besides the wheel would account for these differences?

The wheel has been called the greatest of man's inventions, and records of its use date back about 3,500 years. Much of our technology today depends on the wheel. Make a list of the items you use every day. Which items would be available without the wheel? (Bear in mind that many items, e.g. a pencil, depend on the use of wheels in their manufacture.)

2.   In 1760, after the conquest of New France by Britain, the French Canadians were cut off from all contact with their mother country, France. In what ways were the relations between British and French different from the relations between the French settlers and the Indians?

The fact was that an English society had closed around the [French] Canadians without absorbing them; it had been created against them and it developed without them. Generations of [French] Canadians succeeded one another in a British empire, a British continent, a British state. The political institutions and the economic conditions in which they lived out their lives were British; the social framework built around and above them could not be other than foreign to them.

Guy Frégault, *Canada: The War of the Conquest*, Oxford University Press, p. 342.

Why have the French Canadians clung to their language and customs? List some historical, geographical, and cultural factors to account for this. Why have their language and customs stayed alive in a country where the majority of the people speak English, while the Indian way of life has been largely destroyed?

Explain why some French Canadians are separatists or in sympathy with the separatists today. What historical reasons do the separatists give for the difficulties facing French Canadians today? How do the difficulties faced by the French Canadians differ from the difficulties faced by Indians today? Why do both groups consider their cultures so important?

3. The St Lawrence River has played a major role in the history of Canada, and one of our foremost historians, Donald Creighton, has written a book entitled *The Empire of the St Lawrence*. What part did the St Lawrence play in the discovery of what was eventually to become Canada in the sixteenth and seventeenth centuries? Why was the river so important to the settlers in New France? What part did the river play in the settlement of Upper Canada? During the nineteenth century many canals and locks were built, e.g. the Welland Canal. Why were they built? What role did they play in the economic development of Canada?

The St Lawrence Seaway was built in the twentieth century. What developments in the technology of transportation caused Canada and the U.S. to undertake its construction?

Why is there more cargo tonnage going down the St Lawrence than up? What types of cargo would be going in each direction? What do the figures on traffic to and from Canada and the U.S. show about our trade relations with the U.S.? What do the figures on foreign imports and exports show about our position as a world trading nation?

Table 1

(Combined traffic of the Montreal–Lake Ontario Section and the Welland Canal, with duplications eliminated.)

| | *Upbound* | | *Downbound* | |
| | *1970* | | *1970* | |
	No. of transits	Cargo tons	No. of transits	Cargo tons
Type of Vessel				
Ocean				
Cargo	997	5,406,133	1,022	7,974,311
Tanker	77	590,172	74	321,529
Inland				
Cargo	2,182	17,826,587	2,166	33,656,805
Tug and barge	48	56,220	54	99,927
Tanker	710	3,478,381	728	807,253
Coastal				
Cargo	63	260,753	63	260,386
Tug and barge	67	144,474	57	124,857
Tanker	14	101,698	7	4,186
Non-cargo				
Tug and barge	96	—	89	—
All other[1]	288	—	313	—
Totals	4,542	27,864,418	4,573	43,249,254
Type of Cargo				
Bulk	2,002	22,638,877	2,787	40,643,347
General	717	4,621,019	197	997,439
Mixed	213	614,522	363	1,608,468
Passengers	83	—	82	—
In Ballast				
Ocean	144	—	78	—
Laker	1,063	—	713	—
Coastal	19	—	33	—
Other	301	—	320	—
Type of Traffic				
Domestic				
Canada to Canada	1,536	7,326,601	1,866	15,000,107

	Upbound 1970		Downbound 1970	
	No. of transits	Cargo tons	No. of transits	Cargo tons
Canada to United States	1,573	14,217,606	9	22,356
United States to Canada	13	42,455	1,243	19,278,581
United States to United States	345	281,451	358	652,370
Foreign				
Canada				
Import	211	813,677	—	—
Export	—	—	259	1,149,468
United States				
Import	864	5,182,628	—	—
Export	—	—	838	7,146,372

¹Includes naval vessels
Canada Year Book, 1972.

III

HORSES AND COACHES

1. Were roads more necessary or less necessary in Upper Canada than in Lower Canada? Why? Yonge Street was opened from Toronto to Lake Simcoe in 1795; by 1801 two-thirds of the lots along it were occupied. The photos below are aerial views of a section of Highway 401 near Toronto, taken fifteen years apart. Highway 401 was built as a by-pass to Toronto. What do these photos show about the development of settlement today? How do the reasons for the development along Yonge Street at the end of the eighteenth century compare with the reasons for development along Highway 401 today?

In what ways did the lack of transportation affect the way the Loyalists had to live? On the later aerial photo of Highway 401, pick out some new features designed to serve the community in this area.

Apart from Highway 401 itself, what changes in transportation routes are there in the later photo?

2. Why did the settlers not build good roads for themselves? Why did they resent paying tolls? At a time when there was so much community spirit and neighbours got together for barn-raising bees, why did neighbours not get together for road-building bees?

How are the roads in your province built, operated, and maintained? How is the money collected to pay for roads? In a country where freedom of the individual is so much prized, why do we have the

community as a whole operate some services? List other services that are provided by the community today. What other services do you think should be provided by the community?

Have we lost the community spirit that the early settlers had? Suggest ways in which a greater community spirit might solve some of our problems today.

3. What does the quotation on p. 44 show about the settlers' attitude to forest fires? It has been estimated that a settler was lucky to clear two-to-three acres of farm land annually; the work of clearing, together

with the struggle to prevent the forest taking over again, meant that it could take a settler's whole life to clear a farm of any size. Do you think this explains the settlers' attitude to forest fires? What effect did the apparently unlimited land for settlement have on their attitude? How might the growth of the timber trade have affected the attitude to forest fires?

Great forest fires were first recorded in Canada by the missionaries in the 1600s. The first fire-prevention legislation in Ontario was passed in 1878, and the first fire rangers were appointed in 1886. But despite the provision of fire-fighting services, there have been bad forest fires in this century. One occurred on July 11, 1911. It was called the Porcupine fire, and raged over 500,000 acres. (An acre is about the size of four or five city lots, or two cottage lots.) The fire wiped out all or part of Timmins, South Porcupine, Porquis Junction, and Cochrane. Seventy-three people were reported missing. The Haileybury fire, which occurred on October 4, 1922, burned the equivalent of 18 townships, killed 43 people, and wiped out the homes and belongings of 6,000 others.

What aspects of Canada's climate make forest fires possible? What is the season for forest fires? Describe modern developments in transportation that have aided in detecting and fighting forest fires.

IV

ROADS AND VILLAGES

1.

Table 2   INDUSTRY IN CANADA WEST (ONTARIO)

	Saw mills	Grist mills	Woollen mills	Foundries
1830-51	1,567	692	74	97

Table 3   OCCUPATIONS IN CANADA WEST (ONTARIO), 1861

Advocates, barristers, etc.	632
Blacksmiths	5,431
Boat and bateau men	68
Boot and shoe makers	6,270
Carpenters	9,866
Carters	604

164

Clergymen, priests and ministers	1,716
Clerks	4,262
Coopers	1,798
Dentists	114
Farmers	132,064
Fishermen	258
Grocers	1,010
Inn-keepers	1,568
Labourers	96,543
Lumbermen	4,114
Machinists	614
Manufacturers	253
Masons	1,650
Mechanics	700
Merchants	586
Millers	1,816
Notaries	32
Physicians and surgeons	886
Railroad employees	855
Shopkeepers	3,661
Tailoresses	237
Tailors	2,739
Teachers, female	1,119
Teachers, male	2,956
Traders	168
Saddlers and harness-makers	1,152
Waggon and cart makers	1,509
Weavers	1,110

Census of Canadas, 1860-1, vol. I (Quebec, 1863) , pp. 534-75 *passim.*

What does Table 2 show about the factors that determined the location of a settlement in nineteenth-century Ontario? Table 3 shows that farmers and labourers were the largest percentage of the work force in 1861. Explain how the other occupations supported or depended on farming. What does Table 3 show about social life in 1861?

Table 4   WHEAT GROWN IN CANADA WEST (ONTARIO)
                    (thousands of bushels)

1842	1848	1851	1861	1871
3,222	7,559	12,683	24,620	14,233

Ontario farmers practised wheat farming at first. During the course of the nineteenth century, farming became more diversified and farmers practised mixed farming. Eventually farmers were able to specialize in what was best for the land and the climate in their part of Ontario. Name some examples of specialized farming in Ontario today. Investigate the effects of settlement and better transportation on farming. How are these two developments related? How might these developments have changed the list of occupations in Table 3?

2.

Table 5   CANADA'S METROPOLITAN AREAS

Name	Site	First Settlement	First Role
Calgary	River	1875	Police Post
Edmonton	River	1795	Fur Trade Post
Halifax	Ocean Port	1749	Settlement Node (English)
Hamilton	Lake Port	1778	Settlement Node
Kitchener	River	1800	Settlement Node
London	River	1826	Settlement Node
Montreal	River Port	1642	Fort and Settlement Node (French)
Ottawa	River	1826	Lumbering Town
Quebec	River Port	1608	Fort and Settlement Node (French)
Regina	Creek	1882	Capital for Northwest Territories
St John's	Ocean Port	1600	Fishing Port
Saint John	River Port	1783	Settlement Node (Loyalist)
Saskatoon	River	1883	Settlement Node
Toronto	Lake Port	1750	Fur Trade Post
Vancouver	Ocean Port	1827	Fur Trade Post
Victoria	Ocean Port	1843	Fur Trade Post
Windsor	River Port	1750	Settlement Node (French)
Winnipeg	River	1811	Fur Trade Post

Of the cities listed in Table 5, how were the sites related to the first role? What does the table show about transportation in Canada in the seventeenth, eighteenth, and nineteenth centuries? What factors caused these settlements to grow into large cities?

In recent years, in an attempt to solve the overcrowding in big cities, new planned towns have been built outside the city area. One such is Bramalea outside Toronto. It was started in 1959 to provide a complete community: houses, schools, shopping centres, churches, public buildings such as libraries, recreation areas, and industries to provide employment. Within ten years the population had grown to 16,000 and many of the residents commuted to Toronto to work. Investigate the advantages and disadvantages of living in a planned community like Bramalea. If you planned your own community, how would it differ from where you live now?

3. In the early days many settlements were without newspapers until the community had grown large enough to support one profitably. The following quotation illustrates what it was like when news from the outside world did not penetrate into a community. A resident of Dawson City had obtained an out-of-date Vancouver newspaper and had interested bystanders in its contents by reading passages out loud.

The reader of the war extract, after finishing its persual, announced that the rest of the paper would be read in a hall nearby—admittance 1 dollar! In fifteen minutes the place was thronged at that price with 500 men who patiently stood for over an hour while the enterprising owner read to them accidents, suicides, telegrams, advertisements, and all that goes to make up the life of a Vancouver daily newspaper. For three weeks not one newspaper had appeared in Dawson, and in our sudden isolation the craving for news was as the craving for food. We had something besides mines to talk about for the rest of the day.

Jeremiah Lynch, *Three Years in the Klondike*, London, 1904, p. 38.

Table 6

NUMBER OF PERIODICALS IN BRITISH NORTH AMERICA, 1857–1900
(Includes territory of present-day Canada)

Periodicals	1864	1874	1881	1891	1900
	No.	No.	No.	No.	No.
Dailies	23	46	61	91	121
Tri-weeklies (three times a week)	27	—	11	7	6
Semi-weeklies (twice a week)	16	—	22	17	48
Weeklies	226	330	413	580	804
Bi-weeklies and semi-monthlies (once every two weeks and twice a month)	6	—	10	20	36
Monthlies	27	41	58	119	202

The development of transportation and communication facilities helped newspapers both to gather news and to distribute the papers more effectively. How would the increased availability of newspapers affect people's attitudes to the world outside their community? How might it have affected methods of political campaigning at election time? What do you consider to be the most effective method of political campaigning today? Why?

Where did people find their entertainment in the early settlements? How has this changed in country areas today? Describe the way forms of entertainment depend on the availability of transportation and communication facilities. Is it only improvements in transportation and communication that account for the changes in our entertainment habits, or have people changed? Are these changes for the better?

V

RAILS AND STEAM

1. The first Canadian railway, built to bypass the Richelieu Rapids in Lower Canada, was constructed in 1837. The first major railroad was built in the 1850s and ran from Montreal to Sarnia. The Grand Trunk Railway was completed between Toronto and Montreal in 1856, extended to Sarnia in 1859, and to Rivière du Loup in 1860. The International Railway was begun in 1854 and completed between Halifax and Rivière du Loup in 1873. In Ontario and Quebec there were 1,800 miles of railway by 1860; 5,000 miles by 1875; and 10,000 miles by 1885.

Using a topographical map, plot the course of a railroad in your area. What factors might have influenced the route chosen for the railroad? If possible, compare the original course of the railroad with its present course.

Since the days of the early wood-burning engines, technological advances led first to the introduction of steam engines, then to diesel and electric engines, and recently to experiments with turbine propulsion. In some parts of the world experiments have been conducted with high-speed railways travelling at well over 100 m.p.h. How might these developments have affected the course of railroad lines?

2.   In 1962 the Trans-Canada Highway was completed across mainland Canada, and across Newfoundland in 1965. It took about thirty years to complete and to surface all parts of it, at a cost of nearly $700 million, $400 million of which was contributed by the federal government. The highway parallels the route of the Canadian Pacific Railway nearly all the way from Vancouver to Saint John, New Brunswick, and Moncton. Why was construction of the highway undertaken? Why was this route chosen? What effect might the construction of the highway have had on the Canadian Pacific Railway? During the long period of construction certain parts of the highway were rerouted or straightened. What were the reasons for these changes?

In 1962 construction was begun on the 432-mile Great Slave Lake Railway from Roma, Alberta, to Great Slave Lake.

Construction of the [Great Slave Lake] railway was greatly aided by its proximity to the Mackenzie Highway. For example, in one instance a 46-ton locomotive was transported by truck over the highway for 143 miles farther north to allow for simultaneous construction of the Pine Point spur. General ease of access to the site of railway construction from the highway played a large part in facilitating communication and movement of supplies, thereby keeping the construction of the project running smoothly. . . . Construction of this railway into the Northwest Territories brings two important considerations into focus. First, the selected location along an established communication route points to rail transport as a superior form of overland transport for bulk shipments of minerals and other products. It may be argued that the southbound freight could be transported over the highway, but if so, would the costs be sufficiently low to make the northern products competitive? The decision to build the railway virtually alongside a good existing highway indicates that the highway is unsuitable to meet the ultimate needs of northern development.

Second, construction of the railway has moved the 'jumping-off' point for northern exploration and development 400 miles farther north.

Extract from A. Dubnie and W. Keith Buck, 'Progress of Mineral Development in

Northern Canada', *Polar Record*, Vol. 12, (81), 1965, pp. 683-4.

Why was the Mackenzie Highway constructed? Why was the Great

Slave Lake Railway constructed? In what ways were these reasons different from the reasons for constructing railways in the nineteenth century? Is there any connection between settlement and the construction of the Great Slave Lake Railway? Why did the railway follow the road in this case? Explain the comment in the quotation about making northern products competitive. What products are referred to here?

VI

TRAINS AND TOWNS

1. It has been said that Canada is a nation in defiance of its geography. Examine the main transportation links on a map of Canada. In what direction do they run? Which of the following two passages do you agree with?

Whoever wishes to know what Canada is, and to understand the Canadian question, should begin by turning to the political and natural map. The political map displays a vast and unbroken area of territory, extending from the boundary of the United States up to the North Pole, and equalling or surpassing the United States in magnitude. The physical map displays four separate projections.... The four vary greatly in size, and one of them is very large.... Between the divisions of the Dominion there is hardly any natural trade.... Whether the four blocks of territory constituting the Dominion can forever be kept by political agencies united among themselves and separate from their continent, of which geographically, economically, and with the exception of Quebec ethnologically, they are parts, is the Canadian question....

Goldwin Smith, *Canada and the Canadian Question*, Toronto, 1891. Extract from p. 1.

Canada emerged as a political entity with boundaries largely determined by the fur trade. These boundaries included a vast north temperate land area extending from the Atlantic to the Pacific and dominated by the Canadian Shield. The present Dominion emerged not in spite of geography but because of it. The significance of the fur trade consisted in its determination of the geographic framework. Later economic developments in Canada were profoundly influenced by this background....

H. A. Innis, *The Fur Trade in Canada*, University of Toronto Press, 1956, p. 388.

What part did the railroad play in Confederation? Why did British

Columbia insist upon the building of the railroad as a condition of entering Confederation? If British Columbia had not joined Confederation, could it have remained a British colony? Estimate from a world map the distance of British Columbia from Britain. What problems would British Columbia have faced as a British colony?

The railroad was intended to be a unifying force in Canada. How would it have functioned in that capacity? If the existence of the railroad was intended to cement Canada's hold on the West, do you think it has been a success in light of the West's alienation from eastern Canada? What are the reasons for that alienation?

Explain why means of communication and travel are necessary in holding a nation together. Today radio and TV can travel across international frontiers. What effect are American stations having on Canada?

2. Approximate population of Winnipeg:

1871	700
1872	1,600
1873	3,500
1874	5,000

Price of lots in Winnipeg:

	1871	*1874*	
H.B.Co's Estate	$1,000	$2,000	(Lay in the triangle formed by the Red and Assiniboine Rivers and Portage Avenue.)
McDermot Estates	75	300	
Morris Estate	50	200	(Lay on the opposite side of Main Street from the Red River.)
Schultz Estate	50	300	

From a map of Winnipeg, suggest why the price of land in the areas shown on the table increased so much in such a short time. Why did the population increase so rapidly in the same period? Are these two tables related in any way? What use is made of the land in this area of Winnipeg today? Where is the business district in Winnipeg today? Why do you think it is located there? Where are the residential areas? Where do you think is the most expensive land in Winnipeg today?

Look at the real estate pages of your local newspaper. Try to find ads for similar houses in different parts of the city or town. How do the prices compare? How often is access to a transportation route mentioned

A page from Eaton's 1910 catalogue.

in these ads? Why? If you were going to look for a new home, what factors about its location would be important to you? Would you like to live near a railway? Why?

3. Eaton's opened its first store in 1869 in Toronto. The first mail-order catalogue was published in 1884 and contained 32 pages. Who would likely be buying from this catalogue? Why was mail-order buying possible at this time? In 1905 Eaton's opened their second store—in Winnipeg. By 1916 Winnipeg was the centre of the mail-order operation for the whole of western Canada. Why was Winnipeg chosen rather than another western city? The Winnipeg version of the catalogue differed from the Toronto catalogue. Why would buyers in different parts of the country want different things?

City dwellers as well as people living in isolation now buy from the catalogue. Why? What developments in communication and transportation facilities have made mail-order buying possible? If you could obtain only food from stores, would you be able to obtain everything else you needed from a catalogue? Would you prefer this to going shopping?

Men's Reefers, Mackinaw Coats, Oil Clothing, Etc.

REEFERS—Sizes 34 to 44.

190. Men's Reefers, made of nice quality beaver cloth, navy blue, as cut 190 (coat only) **7.50**

200. Reefers made of navy blue English nap cloth, as cut 200 (coat only) **3.95**

201. Nice quality of Imported Nap Cloth, dark navy blue, as cut 200 (coat only) **5.00**

202. Dark Blue Beaver Cloth Reefer, (coat only), as cut 200 .... **4.50**

203. Men's Reefers (coat only), made of Oxford grey frieze cloth, as cut 200 .... **4.50**

204. Heavy Oxford Grey Harris Frieze Reefer (coat only) as cut 200 .... **6.50**

205. Blue Beaver Cloth Pea Jackets, good linings, as cut 200 .... **7.50**

206. Navy Blue Nap Reefers, English cloth, heavy and warm, as cut 200 (coat only) **8.00**

207. Oxford Grey Irish Frieze Reefers, as cut 200 (coat only) **7.50**

MACKINAW COATS—Sizes 36 to 44.

215. Men's Mackinaw Jackets, unlined, good weight, as cut 215 .... **4.00**

216. Men's Mackinaw Trousers to match above coats, per pair **3.00**

230. Bird's Mackinaw Jackets, blue, black, four pockets and belt, as cut 230 .... **5.00**

231. Bird's Mackinaw Trousers, heavy and warm, per pair **3.50**

232. Short Trousers, knee length, made of Bird's Mackinaw cloth, per pair **3.00**

OIL CLOTHING—Sizes 36 to 44.

250. Fishermen's Oiled Short Jackets in black or yellow, as cut 250, each **1.25**

251. Apron Pants, in black or yellow oiled drill, as cut 250, per pair **1.25**

252. Long Oiled Coats, reach below knee, in yellow or black, each **2.50**

253. Fishermen's Heavy Oiled Capes, each **1.50**

254. Sou'wester Caps, in black or yellow, (as shown on cut 250), each .... **.50**

255. Pommel Slickers, made of yellow oiled drill, each **3.50**

LEATHER COATS—Sizes 36 to 44.

265. Black Leather Coat, small corduroy collar, as cut 265 (coat only) **4.50**

266. Soft Black Leather, lined with strong corduroy as cut 265, (coat only) **5.00**

267. Black Leather Reversible Jackets, corduroy one side, two pockets each side, as cut 265 (coat only) **6.00**

268. Extra Quality of Black Leather, reversible, corduroy lined, three pockets either side, as cut 265 .... **7.00**

269. Tan Leather Coats, reversible, lined with corduroy, as cut 265 (coat only) **6.50**

270. Napa Tan Leather Reversible Jackets, corduroy lined, three pockets either side, as cut 265 (coat only) **9.00**

271. Black Leather Coats, double breasted, lamb lined, high storm collar of wombat fur **11.95**

LAMB LINED AND DUCK JACKETS.
Sizes 36 to 44.

280. Heavy Duck Jackets in black or brown, rubberized check linings (coat only), as cut 280 .... **3.00**

281. Heavy Brown Duck Jackets, storm collar, cuff in sleeve, wool mackinaw lined, as cut 280 (coat only) **4.00**

282. Brown or Black Duck Jackets, single breasted, rubber lined **1.75**

283. Light Tan Duck Shooting Jacket, two large game pockets, seven outside pockets **2.50**

284. Single Breasted Brown Duck Shooting Jacket, two large pockets, rubberized throughout **2.50**

285. Lamb Skin Lined Coats, brown duck outside, corduroy storm collar, cuff in sleeve, as cut 280 (coat only) **4.50**

286. Heavy Brown Duck Jacket, lined with lamb skin, pockets bound with leather, six inch storm collar, as cut 280 .... **6.50**

287. Long Brown Duck Ulster, lamb lined, snap fasteners, storm collar of Lamb skin, cuff in sleeve, fly front, leather bound pockets **11.95**

Eaton's catalogue, 1905-06, Winnipeg edition.

Men's Waterproof Coats and Raincoats

1121

1140

1130

1120

1110

Rubberized Waterproof Coats, Sizes 34 to 44 Chest Measure

1110. Men's Rubberized Waterproof Coats, dark grey or dark fawn English covert cloths, as cut 1110... **3.95**

1111. Men's Covert Cloth Waterproofs, dark grey Herringbone effect, rubber faced bottoms, as cut 1110.. **5.00**

1112. Men's Rubberized Waterproof Coats in English Covert Cloths, plain dark Oxford grey, also black and grey striped effect, rubber faced bottoms, checked linings, as cut 1110.. **6.50**

1113. Men's Covert Cloth Waterproof Coats, Rubberized, in black ground with faint broken stripe of grey running through it, very dressy, as cut 1110.. **8.00**

1114. Imported English Covert Cloth, plain dark grey, checked linings, as cut 1110.. **8.00**

1115. English Covert Cloth, dark olive with check effect, plaid linings, as cut 1110.. **8.00**

1116. Imported Rubberized Coats, olive and Oxford grey in Herringbone stripe effect, as cut 1110.. **10.00**

1117. Heavy English Tweed, grey ground with overcheck, plaid linings, as cut 1110.. **10.50**

1118. Covert Cloth Coats, dark Oxford grey, shoulders and sleeves lined with satin, as cut 1110.. **12.50**

1120. Double Breasted Rubberized Coats, Oxford grey covert cloth, as cut 1120.... **5.00**

Men's Automobile Waterproof Coats

1121. Automobile Waterproof Coats, black vulcanized rubber on outside (giving appearance of leather) with blue Melton cloth on inside, as cut 1121.. **10.00**

1122. Men's Leather Automobile Coats, green flannel lined, wind cuff, cloth motor collar, vent in back, double breasted.................... **20.00**

1123. Fine Danish Leather Waterproof Automobile Coats, leather motor collar, checked wool worsted linings, wind cuffs, double breasted.. **40.00**

Raincoats, Sizes 34 to 44

1130. Cravenette Raincoats, made of dark Oxford grey cloth, as cut 1130.............. **8.00**

1131. Raincoats, imported English cravenette cloths, in olive and grey overplaid effects, as cut 1130.. **12.50**

1132. Cravenette Raincoats, dark Oxford grey and olive cloths, as cut 1130.............. **13.50**

1133. Fancy Cravenette Cloth Rainproof Coats, in neat mixtures with overplaid effects, as cut 1130.. **15.00**

1134. Priestley's Genuine Imported Cloths, Oxford grey and olive shade, as cut 1130 **16.50**

1140. Dark Oxford Grey and olive shade of cravenette cloth, as cut 1140.............. **9.00**

1141. Cravenette Cloths, olive and Oxford grey shades, nicely made, as cut 1140.......... **10.50**

Dull Finished Rubber Coats

1142. Men's and Youth's Dull Finished Rubber Coat, sizes 36 to 44.................... **2.00**

1143. Heavy Dull Finished Drill Sheeting Coats, snap and ring fasteners, sizes 36 to 44.. **3.00**

1144. Extra Heavy, Firemen's Sheeting Dull Rubber Coats, snap and ring fasteners, sizes 36 to 44.. **4.50**

Boys' Waterproofs

1145. Boys' Dull Finished Rubber Coats, to fit boys 4 to 14 years........................ **1.75**

1146. Rubberized Covert Cloth Waterproof Coats, for boys, Oxford grey with checked linings, velvet collar....................

24	26	28	30	32	34
3.50	3.75	4.00	4.25	4.50	4.75

1147. Cravenette Raincoats, in grey and fawn shades, long, loose back with belt...........

23	24, 25	26, 27	28, 29	30, 31	32, 33
5.25	5.50	5.75	6.00	6.25	6.50

Eaton's catalogue, 1905-06, Toronto edition.

VII

CARTS AND BOATS

1.

Table 7   POPULATION OF CANADA

1901	*1911*	*1921*	*1931*	*1941*	*1951*	*1961*
5,371,315	7,206,643	8,787,949	10,376,786	11,506,655	14,009,429	18,238,247

Table 8   ORIGINS OF POPULATION, 1871–1951

	British	*Other* European	Asiatic	Other
1871	2,110,502	1,322,813	4	52,442
1881	2,548,514	1,598,386	4,383	173,527
1901	3,063,195	2,107,327	23,731	177,062
1911	3,999,081	3,006,502	43,213	157,847
1921	4,868,738	3,699,846	65,914	153,451
1931	5,381,071	4,753,242	84,548	157,925
1941	5,715,904	5,526,964	74,064	189,723
1951	6,709,685	6,872,889	72,827	354,028

In the last (1971) census it was found that Canada's population had reached approximately 22½ million. Only a very small fraction of this figure represents the original people of Canada, the Indians and the Eskimos. Consequently the majority of the population are immigrants or the descendants of immigrants. What effect do you think this has had on the development of a Canadian identity?

It would be true to say that immigration was a major source of population increase in Canada. Try to account for the years of relatively high or relatively low immigration in Table 9 by reference to world events. For example, why was there a very high immigration in the years 1910–13 and a very sharp drop in 1915? Why was immigration so low from 1931 to 1944? Why were there so many immigrants in 1957? From what parts of the world did people come to Canada in the peak years of immigration?

During the late nineteenth and early twentieth centuries the government advertised abroad to obtain immigrants for Canada. Why? In the

Table 9   IMMIGRATION TO CANADA, 1852–1970

1852	29,307	1882	112,458	1912	375,756	1942	7,576
1853	29,464	1883	133,624	1913	400,870	1943	8,504
1854	37,263	1884	103,824	1914	150,484	1944	12,801
1855	25,296	1885	79,169	1915	36,665	1945	22,722
1856	22,544	1886	69,152	1916	55,914	1946	71,719
1857	33,854	1887	84,526	1917	72,910	1947	64,127
1858	12,339	1888	88,766	1918	41,845	1948	125,414
1859	6,300	1889	91,600	1919	107,698	1949	95,217
1860	6,276	1890	75,067	1920	138,824	1950	73,912
1861	13,589	1891	82,165	1921	91,728	1951	194,391
1862	18,294	1892	30,996	1922	64,224	1952	164,498
1863	21,000	1893	29,633	1923	133,729	1953	168,868
1864	24,779	1894	20,829	1924	124,164	1954	154,227
1865	18,958	1895	18,790	1925	84,907	1955	109,946
1866	11,427	1896	16,835	1926	135,982	1956	164,857
1867	10,666	1897	21,716	1927	158,886	1957	282,164
1868	12,765	1898	31,900	1928	166,783	1958	124,851
1869	18,630	1899	44,543	1929	164,993	1959	106,928
1870	24,706	1900	41,681	1930	104,806	1960	104,111
1871	27,773	1901	55,747	1931	27,530	1961	71,689
1872	36,578	1902	89,102	1932	20,591	1962	74,586
1873	50,050	1903	138,660	1933	14,382	1963	93,151
1874	39,373	1904	131,252	1934	12,476	1964	112,606
1875	27,382	1905	141,465	1935	11,277	1965	146,758
1876	25,633	1906	211,653	1936	11,643	1966	194,743
1877	27,082	1907	272,409	1937	15,101	1967	222,876
1878	29,807	1908	143,326	1938	17,244	1968	183,974
1879	40,492	1909	173,694	1939	16,994	1969	161,531
1880	38,505	1910	286,839	1940	11,324	1970	147,713
1881	47,991	1911	331,288	1941	9,329		

1970 Immigration Statistics, Department of Manpower and Immigration, p. 4. Reproduced by permission of Information Canada.

light of the figures in Table 9, how successful do you think the government's advertising was? Recently the government has attempted to regulate immigration. Judging by Table 9, how successful has the government been? Why have there been so many illegal immigrants in recent years?

Table 10

INTENDED DESTINATION OF POST-WAR IMMIGRANTS, 1946–1970

Province	
Newfoundland	10,908
Prince Edward Island	4,259
Nova Scotia	48,516
New Brunswick	27,850
Quebec	691,456
Ontario	1,800,172
Manitoba	142,489
Saskatchewan	73,337
Alberta	237,067
British Columbia	372,147
Yukon and N.W.T.	2,773
Not specified	3,883

1970 Immigration Statistics, Department of Manpower and Immigration, p. 24.

Table 11

INTENDED OCCUPATIONAL GROUPS OF POST-WAR IMMIGRANTS, 1946–1970

Managerial	28,480
Professional	278,053
Clerical	191,199
Transportation trades	30,367
Communication trades	6,346
Commercial sales workers	63,012
Financial sales workers	4,375
Service and recreational workers[1]	208,885
Farmers	197,080
Construction trades	151,897
Fishers, trappers, loggers	16,150
Miners	16,645
Manufacturing and mechanical trades	399,175
Labourers	162,739
Others	18,222
Total	1,772,625

[1]Includes domestic servants 128,826
1970 Immigration Statistics, Department of
Manpower and Immigration, p. 75.

177

Explain why immigration varies from province to province in Table 10. How does this compare with the pattern of immigration in the nineteenth century? What does Table 11 tell you about occupations in Canada today? How do the occupations listed in this table compare with the opportunities open to immigrants in the nineteenth century? (See Table 3.)

The following is an excerpt from the Canadian Immigration Regulations of October 1, 1967.

A SUMMARY

These regulations are applied universally and, for the first time, spell out in detail the principles governing the selection of Canadian immigrants. They provide an assessment system which permits immigration officers to apply the same standards in selecting immigrants in all areas of the world. . . .

The regulations created three categories of immigrants: (1) sponsored dependents, (2) nominated (i.e., non-dependent) relatives, and (3) independent applicants who are neither sponsored nor nominated. Dependents are defined for immigration purposes as husband or wife; fiancé or fiancée; unmarried sons or daughters under twenty-one; parents or grandparents over sixty, or younger if they are widowed or unable to work; and orphaned brothers, sisters, nephews, nieces, or grandchildren under eighteen. Provision is also made for adopted children, and in cases where the only dependent is a husband or wife, for the nearest living relative.

Sponsored dependents are admitted to Canada, provided they are in good health and of good character. Independent applicants and nominated relatives

have to meet certain standards under an assessment system based on the following factors.

ASSESSMENT SYSTEM

To qualify for admission, the independent applicant must normally obtain fifty out of the hundred assessment units available. . . .

1. *Education and Training*: Up to twenty assessment units to be awarded on the basis of one unit for each successful year of formal education or occupational training.

2. *Personal Assessment*: Up to fifteen units on the basis of the immigration officer's assessment of the applicant's adaptability, motivation, initiative, and other similar qualities.

3. *Occupation Demand*: Up to fifteen units if demand for the applicant's occupation is strong within Canada whether the occupation is skilled or unskilled.

4. *Occupational Skill*: Up to ten units for the professional, ranging down to one unit for the unskilled.

5. *Age*: Ten units for applicants under thirty-five with one unit deducted for each year over thirty-five.

6. *Arranged Employment*: Ten units

if the applicant has a definite job arranged in Canada.

7. *Knowledge of French and English*: Up to ten units dependent upon the degree of fluency in French and English.

8. *Relative*: Up to five units if the applicant has a relative in Canada able to help him become established but unprepared or unable to sponsor or nominate him.

9. *Employment Opportunities in Area of Destination*: Up to five units if the applicant intends to go to an area of Canada where there is a generally strong demand for labour.

Does the Assessment system seem fair? In excluding certain people from Canada, what is the government trying to protect? In light of the world's population problem, why can not Canada allow unlimited immigration when we have so much land in relation to our population? What are the problems of allowing immigration from over-populated countries only? In light of our unemployment figures, do you think Canada should stop immigration completely? Allow immigration only to those provinces where employment is low? How would you feel if you were out of work? How would you feel if you were an employer and could not get enough people to work in your factory?

2.

Table 12 POPULATION OF WESTERN PROVINCES, 1901–1961

	1901	*1911*	*1921*	*1931*	*1941*	*1951*
Manitoba	255,211	461,394	610,118	700,139	729,744	776,541
Saskatchewan	91,279	492,432	757,510	921,285	895,992	831,728
Alberta	73,022	374,295	588,454	731,605	796,169	939,501
British Columbia	178,657	392,480	524,582	694,263	817,861	1,165,210

Table 13 RAILWAY MILES IN OPERATION

1901	*1911*	*1921*	*1931*	*1941*	*1951*
18,000	25,000	39,000	42,000	42,000	43,000

Table 14 WHEAT EXPORTS ($000,000)

1901	*1911*	*1921*	*1931*	*1941*	*1951*
12	53	185	215	162	441

Table 15 AVERAGE SIZE OF FARMS (IN ACRES), PRAIRIE REGION

1901	*1911*	*1921*	*1931*	*1941*	*1951*
279	289	344	381	405	498

179

From a comparison of Tables 12 to 15, what indications are there that the Prairies have become a major wheat-growing area? List other factors that are not shown by these tables.

Explain how the grain is handled from the time it is harvested to the time it is sold. Where are the major markets for Canadian wheat today? What would the pattern of Canada's foreign markets be like if British Columbia had not joined Confederation?

VIII

CARS AND BICYCLES

1.

Table 16

PERCENTAGE OF CANADIAN POPULATION LIVING IN URBAN CENTRES
(excluding Newfoundland 1911–1941)

1911	*1921*	*1931*	*1941*	*1951*	*1961*
41.8	47.4	52.5	55.7	62.4	69.7

Table 17   MOTOR VEHICLE REGISTRATION IN CANADA

1911	*1921*	*1931*	*1941*	*1951*	*1961*
22,000	465,000	1,201,000	1,573,000	2,872,000	5,517,000

Table 18

POPULATION FORECASTS FOR NINE MAJOR CANADIAN CITIES, 1970–2000
(Estimated population in 000's)

Metro Area	*1970*	*1980*	*1990*	*2000*	*% Increase 1970–2000*
Montreal	2,780	3,540	4,380	5,170	86
Toronto	2,530	3,360	4,310	5,250	107
Vancouver	1,000	1,250	1,530	1,800	80

180

Ottawa	560	710	880	1,050	88
Winnipeg	540	600	670	730	35
Hamilton	500	630	770	900	80
Edmonton	470	630	820	1,010	115
Quebec City	470	600	750	880	87
Calgary	390	510	670	820	110
Totals	9,240	12,830	14,780	17,610	90

D. J. Reynolds, *Urban Transport Problems* (Urban Canada, Problems and Prospects. Research Monograph No. 3) , Central Mortgage and Housing Corporation, Ottawa, 1971.

Table 19

CAR OWNERSHIP PER CAPITA IN NINE MAJOR CANADIAN CITIES IN 1965

City	Cars per capita of total population
Montreal	0.24
Toronto	0.34
Vancouver	0.34
Ottawa-Hull	0.28
Winnipeg	0.27
Edmonton	0.28
Hamilton	0.35
Calgary	0.21
Quebec City	0.28

(The cars in this table account for almost half the cars in Canada in 1965.)

Central Mortgage and Housing Corporation, Ottawa, *op. cit.*

Table 20   ESTIMATED AIR POLLUTION IN URBAN CANADA, 1970

Pollutant	Annual output of road vehicles (millions of tons)	Output by other sources (millions of tons)	Totals	% of total	% attributable to road vehicles
Carbon monoxide	3.3	0.4	3.7	40	90
Sulphur oxides	0.1	1.9	2.0	22	5
Hydrocarbons	1.2	0.5	1.7	19	63
Nitrogen oxides	0.3	0.5	0.8	9	38
Particles	0.1	0.8	0.9	10	11
Totals	5.0	4.1	9.1	100	55

Central Mortgage and Housing Corporation, Ottawa, *op. cit.*

181

The private automobile is more predominant in North America than anywhere else. What factors account for this? Has the car contributed to the quality of Canadian life? Would we be suffering from urban sprawl today if the car had not been invented?

Until the car became prevalent, there were few traffic regulations in Canada. Explain the purpose of the many traffic regulations we have today. Given the trends towards population growth, urban living, and car ownership in Canada in the above tables, suggest what traffic regulations might be in force by the year 2001.

Cars create large amounts of pollutants. Yet emission control devices use more fuel and give fewer miles per gallon. Suggest ways of combating this double problem.

If we ran out of oil, could our way of life survive? Why would it not be possible to return to a way of life similar to that of the early settlers in Canada?

2. In an attempt to solve the problem of traffic congestion, the two largest cities in Canada, Toronto and Montreal, have recently built public transit systems. In light of the following two quotations, how successful do you think public transit systems are likely to be in solving the transportation problems of the large city?

One point all [the public transit] systems have in common is that they only make sense for large towns—say, metropolitan areas of at least one half to one million people. Smaller towns do not generate enough traffic even at peak hours to support a mass transit system. Also, these systems work best where the density of population is fairly high in suburban areas; this places larger numbers of people within the 'catchment areas' of the stations, and makes it more likely that use of the system would be high enough for fairly efficient operation. Thus, a mass transit system tends to work best in, and will encourage the development of, centrally organized and more densely populated cities. The automobile in contrast tends to work best in, and favour the development of, multi-centred, low density cities. When cities choose one form of transport system over another, they go a long way towards choosing one basic form of city over another, so great is the interaction between transport and urban form.

An important point is that a good mass transit system in a large city may be of critical importance to the poorer and the older populations of the city. These are the people who cannot afford to own a car or who cannot drive one. In the past, as the automobile has risen to dominance, and transit ridership has declined, so the cost and service aspects of transit have also deteriorated, leaving the poor and old in worse plight than before. In the modern city, these people are less mobile than ever, in contrast with the highly mobile car owners. Finding employment and using services is made difficult for those already disadvantaged. Thus improving the mass transit system of the city is a way to increase the opportunities open to the poor and old, as well as a way of reducing traffic congestion faced by commuters.

John Wolforth and Roger Leigh, *Urban Prospects*, 1971, p. 139. Reprinted by permission of The Canadian Publishers, McClelland and Stewart Limited, Toronto.

In an unexpected reversal of a secular trend the invention of the internal combustion engine has led, during the last 40 years, to a growing displacement of public by private transportation. In both the United States and Canada travel by private automobile now absorbs about 10 per cent of the Gross National Product, and in both coun-

tries accounts for at least 85 per cent of all person-miles in inter-urban travel....

The spread of the private automobile has made the operation of public transit more difficult in three ways. First, by depriving it of a substantial portion of its passengers, it has decreased its vehicle load, necessitating either higher fares or a curtailing of service, or both, leading to a further decrease in passengers. Second, by congesting the street surface which it shares with transit vehicles, it has slowed down transit movement, thereby increasing its cost of operation and decreasing its attractiveness. Third—most fundamental and least understood—the private car has created a pattern of low density development which can no longer be served by public transportation because it becomes impossible to assemble a sufficient payload on any one line.

Hans Blumenfeld, 'Transportation in the Modern Metropolis', *Queen's Quarterly*, Vol. LXVII, No. 4, Winter 1961. Extract reprinted by permission of the author.

What social costs, as well as economic costs, are involved in the provision or lack of public transit systems? Should transit systems be subsidized as a community resource? Should car owners pay additional taxes to support a public transit system?

Used as we are to thinking in terms of 'cities' and 'suburbs', we sometimes fail to grasp the implications of the emergence of a new form of human settlement which is going on before our eyes....

The country-to-city movement of population continues, all over the world, and stronger than ever. But this centripetal wave is now being met by a second, centrifugal 'city-to-suburb' wave. The combined result of these

Sherway Gardens Shopping Plaza in Etobicoke, near Toronto.

two movements is the modern metropolitan area, or 'metropolis' for short, which is emerging as the predominant form of human settlement in every section of the globe, but has developed farthest on the North American continent.

Hans Blumenfeld, 'Transportation in the Modern Metropolis', *Queen's Quarterly*, Vol. LXVII, No. 4, Winter 1961. Extract reprinted by permission of the author.

What implications does the rise of the metropolis have for the development of transportation and public transit systems? Where would you expect metropolises to develop in Canada?

3. The aerial photo shows a new shopping centre recently opened in a Toronto suburb. The centre includes two department stores, two supermarkets, and a great variety of specialty stores. In what ways would the shopping habits of the people in the surrounding area be changed by the opening of such a centre? Estimate the amount of

parking space available, and the approximate number of people the centre could probably accommodate at any time. How far would you be willing to drive to shop at such a centre? Taking that distance as the radius, what area would the centre serve?

How have shopping habits changed from the days of the village store? How often does your family shop at a supermarket, a department store, a specialty shop? Why would there be so many specialty shops in comparison with supermarkets in the shopping centre? What technological changes other than transportation have made these changes in shopping habits possible?

IX

HARVESTERS AND TRUCKS

1.

Table 21   PROPORTION OF CANADIAN POPULATION CLASSIFIED

AS RURAL AND URBAN, CANADA, 1901–1961[1]

	1901	*1911*	*1921*	*1931*	*1941*	*1951*[1]	*1961*	*1971*
Rural	64	55	49	46	47	38	30	24
Urban	36	45	51	54	53	62	70	76

[1]The definition of rural changed between 1941 and 1951. By the 1941 definition, the proportion of rural population would be about 43%. Hence the new definition overstates the actual degree of change.

Decennial Census of Canada 1931, 41, 51, 61, 71.

Table 22

AVERAGE SIZE OF FARMS (IN ACRES), 1901–1961 CANADA

1901	*1911*	*1921*	*1931*	*1941*	*1951*	*1961*
124	160	198	224	237	279	359

Census of Canada, 1961.

Table 23   NUMBER OF TRACTORS ON FARMS, 1921–1960

1921	*1930*	*1940*	*1950*	*1960*
47,455	110,019	146,263	362,929	565,051

Table 24

PROPORTION OF OCCUPIED DWELLINGS WITH SPECIFIED LIVING
CONVENIENCES AND FACILITIES, RURAL FARM, RURAL NONFARM,
AND URBAN, CANADA, 1951–1961

	Passenger car	Inside running water	Bath or shower	Flush toilet	Mechanical refrigerator	Radio & T.V.
Rural Farm						
1951	52.1	32.9	15.5	19.9	21.9	88.6
1961	77.5	60.6	40.4	43.8	80.0	67.3
Rural Nonfarm						
1951	37.8	46.1	27.5	34.7	30.3	85.6
1961	65.6	68.1	49.7	54.3	77.8	67.4
Urban						
1951	40.8	94.1	77.4	85.6	58.8	95.1
1961	67.8	98.3	89.0	90.0	95.8	88.4

Describe the changes in farm life that have occurred during the twentieth century. Explain the difference between rural farm and rural nonfarm in Table 25. Is the rural nonfarm population likely to increase or decrease in the future? Explain how it is possible for the rural population to decline and the size of farms to increase in all regions of Canada. Is it possible for the whole population eventually to become urbanized?

2.

Table 25   RAILROADS, PASSENGERS CARRIED, 1880–1960
(in 000's)

1880	1890	1900	1910	1920	1930	1940	1950	1960
6,463	12,821	21,500	35,900	51,300	34,700	22,000	31,100	19,500

Compare Table 25 with Tables 13 and 17. Explain why the number of passengers declined after the peak year of 1920, and again after 1950.

Table 26   RAILROADS, FREIGHT CARRIED, 1880–1960
(thousands of tons)

1880	1890	1900	1910	1920	1930	1940	1950	1960
9,939	20,787	35,946	74,500	127,400	115,200	110,400	164,400	178,800

Table 27   AVERAGE FREIGHT TONNAGE PER MILE OF LINE,
CANADIAN NATIONAL RAILWAYS
(in thousands)

Period	Branch Lines	Main Lines
1926–35	289	3,162
1936–45	311	3,648
1946–55	418	5,118
1956–59	405	5,858

Report of the Royal Commission on Transportation, Queen's Printer, Ottawa, 1961, Vol. 2, p. 66.

Why have so many branch lines closed, even though freight carried on them has increased? Are the railways justified in closing branch lines?

Why are railways not becoming obsolete? What future might they have, in light of new technological advances in containerization, new kinds of engine propulsion, etc?

3. We have traced the development from paddles to all kinds of wheels in this book, and now we have reached the age of wings.

Table 28   PASSENGERS CARRIED BY AIR, 1920 to 1960

1920	*1930*	*1940*	*1950*	*1960*
15,265	124,875	149,025	1,553,346	5,451,716

How does the direction of the major airline routes across Canada compare with the direction of other forms of transportation? Are the reasons similar in all three cases, bearing in mind that airline travel was only developed in the present century? What deductions can you make about the relation of airline routes to settlement?

Table 29

PERCENTAGE OF PASSENGER MILES TRAVELLED IN CANADA
BY VARIOUS MODES OF TRANSPORTATION, 1968

Cars	Air	Rail	Bus and Urban Public Transit
89%	5%	3%	3%

187

Table 30

COMPARISON OF STANDARD ONE-WAY FARES
AND TIMES IN TRANSIT, 1969

Vancouver to	Rail		Air	
	Fare	*Time*	*Fare*	*Time*
Prince George	16.95	13 hrs. 50 min.	39.00	1 hr. 5 min.
Edmonton	23.00	21 hrs.	36.00	1 hr. 20 min.
Regina	31.00	30 hrs.	65.00	1 hr. 50 min.
Toronto	58.00	70 hrs.	120.00	4 hrs. 5 min.
Montreal	61.00	72 hrs. 30 min.	132.00	5 hrs. 20 min.

H. C. Purdy, *Transport Competition and Public Policy in Canada,* University of British Columbia Press, Vancouver, 1972, p. 94.

Explain the popularity of air travel in light of fares and time taken to travel to a destination. What amount of time should be added to the air times given in Table 29 to give the total picture of travelling time by air? What does the popularity of air travel show about the Canadian standard of living?

Rail companies bear their own indirect costs; most of the indirect costs of highway travel are funded by governments. Does this give trucking companies an unfair advantage over railway companies? Should car owners be taxed more heavily than other citizens to help bear the indirect costs of highways? In what ways are they taxed now?

What do you consider are the relative merits of government subsidies to different forms of transportation, including urban transit systems? In what ways have airlines increased the quality of Canadian life? What are their disadvantages?

IN CONCLUSION

Now that you have read this book, what conclusions can you draw about the relationship of transportation to settlement? About the relationship of the means of transportation to our way of life? We have seen how older methods of transportation fell largely into disuse as new inventions appeared. What effect do you think the development of space travel might have on transportation here on earth?

In 1873 Jules Verne wrote his famous novel *Around the World in Eighty Days*. His ideas seemed fantastic at the time, yet he anticipated many technological inventions of the twentieth century. Find some science-fiction stories that envisage new methods of travel. How do these writers speculate about changes in our way of life? Do you find their ideas fantastic?

A BIBLIOGRAPHICAL NOTE

The following is not a comprehensive bibliography but a note on some of the sources used in this book that might be consulted by those interested in going more deeply into certain aspects of transportation.

Although comparisons between different sets of statistics should be made with caution, their use often sheds light on interrelationships between various factors. The best source of historical statistics is M. C. Urquhart, ed., *Historical Statistics of Canada* (Macmillan, Toronto, 1965).

The standard work on transportation is still G. P. de T. Glazebrook's *History of Transportation in Canada* (McClelland and Stewart, 1938), although of course it does not cover the most recent period. It has been reprinted in two volumes in the Carleton Library *Vol. 1. Continental Strategy to 1867; Vol. 2. National Economy 1867–1936.* For more specialized studies, the most readable account of the building of the CPR is Pierre Berton's two-volume history *The National Dream: The Great Railway* and *The Last Spike* (McClelland and Stewart, 1970 and 1971), while the building of the CNR is fully covered in G. R. Stevens' *History of the Canadian National Railways* (Macmillan, New York, 1973). Those wishing to go more deeply into the economic and governmental aspects of transportation in Canada might consult A. W. Currie,

Canadian Transportation Economics (University of Toronto Press, 1967), H. C. Purdy, *Transport Competition and Public Policy in Canada* (University of British Columbia Press, 1972), and Canada Transport Commission, *Intercity Passenger Transport Study* (Queen's Printer, 1970), but the reader should be warned that these are highly technical works.

Historical geography can contribute many insights to the relationship between transportation and settlement, and R. Cole Harris and John Warkentin, *Canada Before Confederation* (Oxford University Press, 1974) is an extremely useful study of the pre-Confederation period in Canada. It is beyond the scope of this book to give a detailed study of the history of a settlement, but for those wishing to make such a study R. C. Langman's *Patterns of Settlement in Southern Ontario* (McClelland and Stewart, 1971) is a useful book that includes two detailed case studies.

Finally, in addition to the works cited in chapter 8, two books by Eric Winter, *Urban Landscapes* and *Urban Areas* (Bellhaven House, 1969 and 1971), give further useful insights into urban problems.

Acknowledgements

The authors and the publisher wish to acknowledge the kindness of those who granted permission for the reproduction of the copyright illustrations indicated below.

T. EATON COMPANY OF CANADA, ARCHIVES
pp. 172, 173, 174.

GLENBOW-ALBERTA INSTITUTE
p. 33 lower: drawing by George E. Finlay; p. 84: watercolour by Franz Hölzlhuber; p. 86; p. 92: (A. Goodwin estate, Calgary); p. 96; p. 105: drawing by Melton Prior from the *Illustrated London News*; p. 111: drawing by George E. Finlay; p. 114 lower; p. 122: 'Friedland homestead at Vermilion'.

RALPH GREENHILL, TORONTO
p. 62.

HUDSON'S BAY COMPANY
Back cover and p. 15: painting by Franklin Arbuckle.

V. C. LAST, WIARTON, ONTARIO
pp. 60, 144.

LOCKWOOD SURVEY CORPORATION LTD.
pp. 162 and 163.

MASSEY-FERGUSON INDUSTRIES LTD
p. 146.

LARRY MILBERRY, AIR PHOTOS CANADA
pp. 64, 65, 127, 134, 148, 149, 150, 151.

NATIONAL GALLERY OF CANADA
p. 24: 'The Habitant Farm' by C. Krieghoff. Gift of the estate of the Hon. W. C. Edwards, Ottawa, 1928.

NATIONAL MUSEUMS OF CANADA
p. 2; p. 101: Geological Survey.

NOTMAN PHOTOGRAPHIC ARCHIVES, MCCORD MUSEUMS, MCGILL UNIVERSITY
Front cover; pp. 6, 129.

PROVINCIAL ARCHIVES OF MANITOBA
p. 100: from an original oil painting by W. F. Lynn; p. 114 upper; 117, 123.